DARK
Politics

Best wishes,
Ben.

LEVI BRYANT · GEAN MORENO
REZA NEGARESTANI
BENJAMIN NOYS · NICK SRNICEK
CHRISTIAN THORNE
ALEX WILLIAMS · BEN WOODARD

Edited by Joshua Johnson

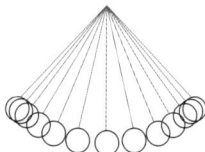

Pendular Sweeps Series

[NAME] Publications
Printed in Hong Kong, 2013
ISBN: 978-0-9840566-9-9

Contents

Introduction

Joshua Johnson

The crisis in contemporary capitalism and the continuing failure of the neoliberal imagination seem to forestall any solutions. Rather than questioning the wisdom of further financialization and deepening inequality, the leading technocrats are embracing austerity and doubling-down on the spirit of market-fundamentalism that lead to the economic crises of 2008 and the ongoing euro-crisis.

The last thirty years of critical theory have also failed to provide a significant challenge to the dogmas of neoliberalism. As market logic has embraced ever widening aspects of the social, the naturalization of capitalism has made the epistemic limits of critical theory ever more apparent. Those theories, as they have clawed at the limits of the social continuum, have ironically succumb to the very economic analysis they were meant to defy - the cost of resistance in the face of dwindling resources not yet subsumed by capital made their claims to real alternatives disappear into a recursively formulated critique. Without a robust consideration the real, or a re-consideration of the Kantian assumptions of access, any escape to beyond the efficacious operativity of capitalism has seemed impossible.

With the rise of Speculative Realism, Object Oriented Ontology, and other realist projects there has been a turn away from anthropo-centrically hardened philosophies of the last thirty years and a re-consideration of the outside. This new perspective entails new resources and complications for any political philosophy, which this compilation explores from a variety of views.

Certainly the question of politics has been central to the spirit of these new philoso-phies from the beginning. A radicalized Deleuzianism, epitomized by the work of Nick Land, but engaged both positively and negatively by many of the contributors in this volume, made the driving forces of capi-talism a central point of contention. The po-litical thesis of Land's work, that capitalism's experimental puissance may be collapsed with an ontologized death-drive which will propel capitalism beyond its own limited political vocabulary, has challenged others to confront new strategies for re-configuring the political imaginary.

Gean Moreno proposes a metaphorical relationship between the apocalyptic sci-fi "grey-goo" nano-tech mythology and capitalism, developing this story to begin to think an alien and othered capitalism whose purposes overlap, but are not necessarily aligned with those of humans. He questions whether the energies unleashed by capitalism might not be simply contingently negated, but diverted into new strategies of resistance.

Benjamin Noys coined the term 'accelerationism' to describe the type of hyper-capitalist logic favored by Land. In The Grammar of Neoliberalism, Noys confronts Land's naturalization of the neoliberal logic. Like Moreno's "grey goo" analogy, Noys' regards Landian acceleration as apocalyptic. Capitalist acceleration exasperates of the hyper-efficiency imposed by market logic and speeds up its processes of 'creative destruction', butchering all elements of the social to fit into the machine logics of market economics. However, as Noys argues, this systematic and mechanistic application of market forces effectively reduces the revolutionary capacity of any agent to another cog in the capitalist machine. The horizon of his or her activity becomes commensurate with that of the neoliberal project itself.

Reza Negarestani's text investigates the strategy of openness and its relationship with death to radicalize the implications of an accelerationist thought. The question of an outside is a central one to a capitalist system which must always posit the affordability of its own horizon in excess of its limits. The capitalist must insist upon the profit as its own transcendental limit, denying openness in favor of an externalized outside to be consumed. Rather than capitalism's creative-destruction, Negarestani examines the process of necrophilia (the becoming of life into death, and death into life) which is never exhausted or contained by any program. Instead of viewing the outside as a raw resource for the expansion of the body of capital, germinal death infects the body of capitalism, turning it into a feast for the unbounded un-life which opens the inside to its continuous extensibility. Capitalism, or any transcendentally limited project, is always subject to trajectories beyond its own ideological value assumptions.

Ben Woodard begins a survey of the contemporary environment, and like Negarestani, questions the opposition between two molar oceanic forces, that of the liquidity of capital and the desiring flows of nature. He characterizes capitalism as a violent masculine force that attempts to hegemonically divert all flows to its purposes, strangling the diversity of the ocean. There is however, the feminist force of the ocean, whose strength lies in the diversity of its experiments, which cannot be contained by the bounds of capitalism's affordability. Woodard proposes that, as theorists, we must decouple the violence and struggle of capitalism from its essential boundedness, and recognize that these strategies are also political tools for the unbounded ocean.

Christian Thorne tackles the problem of essentialism in another way, critiquing the political ontologists who would couple the affective spirit of their political program with being itself. In this we see shades of Noys critique of Land, in which the machinic efficacy of capitalism becomes a deterministic program. Thorne applies the images of water and fire, and shows how a naive ontologization of their qualities as pure necessity leads to theology. He questions whether any speculative ontology can truly escape the epistemic and ideological limits of its author.

Levi Bryant looks at the critique of a political ontology from a different perspective, decoupling the notion of what "is" from what "ought" to be. He argues that philosophers have a responsibility to examine what "is", that is to map the various beings of the world, as they are, whether they agree with our ethics or not. Yet, he also thinks that it is also possible to maintain an ethical-political program that embraces and adapts the various critical perspectives from Marxism, Feminism, etc. to continue to shape the landscape that a considered ontology may uncover.

Nick Srnicek and Alex Williams engage with the form of the manifesto to revive a project of Marxist accelerationism. They critique both the exhaustion of neoliberal ideology and a reactionary leftism, while proposing a new political imaginary. They envision a decoupling of technology from its instrumentalization by capitalism, while demanding a shift away from what they characterize as an ineffective horizontally organized and localized politics. They believe the liberation and utilization of the techno-sciences coupled with a cunning use of politics will revive the political imaginary of the future.

Acknowledgments

To all of the contributors, whose fantastic work and conversation has expanded my horizons, and without whose efforts this volume would not have been possible. Any textual errors are surely due to my own oversight as editor and not the authors' thoughtful contributions. Special thanks to Gean Moreno for taking this on with [NAME] Publications and bringing this volume to print. I also owe him gratitude for his assitance in editing the introduction.

Notes on the Inorganic: Accelerations

Gean Moreno

> Is not the totality of all our endeavors, all our social relations, tending towards the making over of the planet as a total work of art?… What if the work of art into which the world is turned excludes the presence of its own makers? What if its creation destroys the biological possibility of human life on the planet?[1]
>
> -McKenzie Wark

In 1986, K. Erik Drexel, at the time a Research Affiliate at the MIT Artificial Intelligence Laboratory, published *Engines of Creation*, a book celebrating the growing productive capabilities of nanotechnology and the coming age of mechanochemical manufacturing. He was preparing us for the "assembler breakthrough"—the moment in which self-replicating machines the size of molecules would become the driving engines of contemporary technology. Like sci-fi, it was a testament of—or from—the future. It came in a language unequivocally borne on warm currents of affirmation and delight: a less burdensome life was guaranteed by the inevitable emergence of molecular technology. We were moving up, pushing forward, relieving ourselves of unseemly burdens, like those of aging and dying, or of having to work for a living. There is only one chapter in the book—Chapter 11: "Engines of Destruction"—in which Drexel slips out of character. Or, rather, in which a simple and formal warning has enough seductive charge and narrative potential to take on a life of its own. Apparently, it was in the following passage in which Drexler slipped most, if we judge by the disproportionate amount of critical heat it generated from his colleagues:

> The early transistorized computers soon beat the most advanced vacuum-tube computers because they were based on superior devices. For the same reason, early assembler-based replicators could beat the most advanced modern organisms. "Plants" with "leaves" no more efficient than today's solar cells could out-compete real plants, crowding the biosphere with an inedible foliage. Tough omnivorous "bacteria" could out-compete real bacteria: They could spread like blowing pollen, replicate swiftly, and reduce the biosphere to dust in a matter of days. Dangerous replicators could easily be too tough,

small, and rapidly spreading to stop–at least if we make no preparation. We have trouble enough controlling viruses and fruit flies.[2]

The threat that this paragraph relates was known in nanotechnology circles as the "grey goo problem." In the wake of Drexler's book, it became as fashionable and loved among sci-fi writers and aficionados as it grew abhorred by people in the field of nanotechnology. The tale, in a more developed stage, involves swarms of self-replicating, biovorous nano-assemblers run amok. If what it relates was to actually occur, it would be the first and only environmental disaster generated by the field of molecular mechanochemical manufacturing—total consumption of the planet happening in as little as an unfathomable ~104 seconds after the chain of reproduction is triggered.[3] Mimicking biological replicators like bacteria, and having aborted or overstepped the boundaries of the use they were intended for, becoming sentient and cunning (in the sci-fi version), or produced in a lab with the capacity to function autonomously (in the scientist's hypothetical version), these molecular-sized machines multiply exponentially on their own by transferring "genetic" algorithms to new units and using the planet's biosphere as fuel. They reproduce until they ingest all living forms and leave behind a desolate landscape of grey slime. "Ecophagic nanorobots would regard living things as environmental carbon accumulators," writes Robert A. Freitas Jr. , "and biomass as a valuable ore to be mined for carbon and energy. Of course, biosystems from which all carbon has been extracted can no longer be alive but would instead become lifeless chemical sludge."[4]

The world ends, then, as a dead, undifferentiated, slimy surface—a massive lithosphere coated by lifeless sludge and nanomass wreckage. No bang, but also no whimper. Only a hissing out, like the end of an old mixtape. The scenario is one of a mass, if unintentional, "species" suicide (the replibots) and full biological elimination. This is fated by the meeting of an environment with finite energy-producing resources and machines programmed for infinite reproduction and non-mutation. One ecosystem doesn't emerge by eating and metabolizing another—which would just tune this story to the affirmationist escape hatch available to certain flinching strands of apocalyptic sci-fi. This isn't, in the end, a machines-takeover story. It's not the Singularity. These replibots eat the environment for no reason at all except the programmed proliferation of more replibots, unaffected by the useless grey goo they are generating and the acceleration of their own demise that is inevitably lodged in their multiplying numbers. This isn't the production of a new world, but a sped-up, unintentional dissolution of the existing one. One world isn't being transfigured into another; it is being transfigured into a non-world, dissolved into inorganic slime.

Articles challenging this Grey Goo scenario quickly appeared and, as the replibots they targeted, multiplied exponentially. This was hardly surprising. Dependent on large public research grants and seeking application in the private manufacturing sector, the field of nanotechnology quickly deployed its reactive fronts. The last thing it needed was an unsubstantiated speculative doomsday scenario out there in the public imagination to contend with. Drexler himself, after the publication and success of his book, has been at the forefront of efforts to propose that the multiplying replibot scenario is not very likely, and that advances in safety since the book appeared all but guarantee its impossibility.

In the end, the mythological space opened by his gleeful slip into the apocalyptic needed to be fenced off and eradicated because, as Drexel explicitly proposed in his book, giving us a furtive glance at the economic imperative that guides the project of molecular technology, the market is the "ultimate test." And we all know that a capricious market may suddenly recoil from this sort of risk (even if not from others, as we've come to learn lately), particularly where long-term and high-investment projects that involve untested technologies are concerned. But of course what is interesting, beyond just considering the connection of contemporary science to free market, is attempting to account for the reason that this Grey Goo scenario found such warm reception beyond cloistered nanotechnologists, in the culture it was imaginarily decimating and abolishing. Why does the scenario still have currency as narrative, while having been completely debunked as hard science in professional quarters? What amorphous, slippery collective feeling does this scenario serve as outlet or allegory for?

The pages that precede the introduction of the "Grey Goo problem" in Drexel's book are concerned with the range of *eliminations* that will accompany the proliferation of assembler-based replicators. He mentions specifically the elimination of global trade (automated engineering can be localized and shrunken), the elimination of the current parameters of human mortality (the indefinite extension of life through artificial cell-reparation mechanisms), the elimination of human labor due to near absolute automation (replicators producing objects, as well as other replicators to replace and upgrade themselves). All these positively-charged eliminations, however, are secondary to the most terrifying potential consequence of nanotechnology gone awry or mishandled: the abolition of life, the wholesale destruction of the biological.

Beyond whatever kind of warning—fair or exaggerated, indispensable or there simply for effect—it serves as in relation to the real advances of nanotechnology, the "Grey Goo problem" allegorizes eliminative threats to life *that exist on other planes or spheres*. It absorbs threats that we may not be able to deal with directly; threats that need to be displaced in order to keep them from cutting a gash in our symbolic order; threats that may just be too uncomfortable, indict us too shamefully, and demand too much of us in terms of altering our ways of living, to discourage anything but displacement or concealment. Their cut is too deep. The notion that Drexler's apocalyptic scenario is a recoding of different processes of elimination seems a particularly plausible explanation considering just how *unreal* this Grey Goo threat is in the field of nanotechnology, according to the very community of experts that make up the field.

One of the things that the "Grey Goo problem" may *stage* is the very dissipative tendency that is at the core of capitalist production itself—the movement toward resource elimination as the necessary correlation to the systemic expansion of capital. For the capitalist system to sustain itself, to reproduce indefinitely, seemingly forever, it needs to incrementally gobble up more and more; it needs to continually upturn any balanced cycles as these translate into potential stagnation and lost opportunities for growth. The imperative to reproduce and enlarge and the need for unrestricted license to devastate are two sides of the same coin, not only mutually reinforcing but structurally essential. And they are not only deplorable but horrific in an aesthetically generative way: they set us on course to imagine the world as it slides toward the inorganic. There is something in capitalism's constant invasion of resource-rich contexts and its strategies once it settles in that encourages images that project a dead-world as what is left inevitably in its wake. And just as one can imagine (or has seen) patches of devastated and desolate land, a kind of localized post-resource extraction desertification, one can just as easily imagine this becoming a planetary condition. The globe as a rotating, lifeless lithosphere, coated by the fine dust of decomposing once-organic particles.

These days, few would claim to be anything but appalled by the capital's dissipative compulsion. And just as small a number would accept that such an impulse can be easily naturalized as an unproblematic expression of the intrinsic dynamic of rational economic development. The innocence that allows us to be hoodwinked in this way belongs to another time--or at least one hopes it does. The delusional character of a system predicated on the infinite growth can't be smudged out of the picture all that easily anymore. We know that such a system is not viable in the long run, that its predatory practices are indefensible, and yet we continue to behave, at all levels, as if it is a necessary and unshakeable system nonetheless. It's a fatality that we can at most resist through the subtraction of our subjective belief in it, which we often register in private gestures, at reduced scales, with "personal initiative" and demands for "corporate responsibility."

We participate, despite ourselves, in a consensual collective fantasy, frayed at its edges but holding, of plenitude and regeneration, of the miracle of the system's unendingness, assailed on every side by apocalyptic fantasies but nowhere extinguished by them, ratifying the old, and slightly worn by now, Jamensonean/Zizekean quip which says that it is easier to imagine the end of the world than the end of capitalism. In fact, it is Zizek who doesn't tire of reminding us that in our "post-ideological" world we participate fully in the capitalist game while telling ourselves that we don't believe in it at all. We disavow in thought and speech what we adhere to in action.

The naturalization of resource depletion, even if it now registers mostly in (or as) the discrepancy between our actions and our discourses, cannot help but begin to affect cultural production. It stretches from the field of sculpture—marked by the slouching toward interior design and décor—to urban and infrastructural thinking that folds into its concerns the desertified landscapes to come of post-resource depletion. Last year, design research collective InfraNet Lab/ Lateral Office developed a series of speculative infrastructural projects.[5] Among these was *Re-Rigging*, an ambitious proposal which sought to develop offshore oil extraction infrastructure for the Caspian Sea. (Oil extraction is not yet marching at full speed in the Caspian Sea due to post-1991 border and legal disputes, but it is inevitably coming.) The project seeks to produce this infrastructure in such a way that potentials embedded at the design stage in what will eventually be the derelict rigs left behind (oil extraction has been given a very short lifespan in the area, peeking between 2020 and 2030) can be actualized, and the built structures can serve new functions, as recreational sites, bird sanctuaries and the like. What is astonishing in this is that the depletion of fossil fuels in the area is naturalized as empirical fact, as inexpugnable given—as if it had already happened—and design can only begin and be relevant by calculating it into the process. This is the project's pragmatic realism. A coming decimated landscape, the end point of a process that is so natural as to be accounted for before it is even set in motion in this particular instance, becomes a determining factor in the architectural production of the present.

While it is true that Infra Net Lab/Lateral Office is proposing adaptive and reactive systems, laudably serving as counterpoints to the monological infrastructures of the

20th Century which eventually end up as useless concrete carcasses, the first thing it adapts and reacts to is the will to depredation that characterizes transnational capital. This translates into a kind of site or even geographical sensitivity, it's true: infrastructure is not only conceived to exploit one aspect or resource of a place—in this case, the products of the subsea geology—but as an interface between a multiplicity of elements, conditions, and populations. In the Caspian Sea, the infrastructure proposed by Infra Net Lab/Lateral Office will look to intertwine the subsea, the activity in the sea (the need to sustain and enlarge the populations of sturgeon), and what happens in the air (the migratory patterns of birds which cut right over this body of water), while also building into the system the potential to recuperate the infrastructure, as recreational areas and the like, after it can no longer serve its original purpose. The passive anticipation of uselessness that accompanied infrastructural production in the past is swapped for active planning for post-depletion. It's pre-emptive design for the inevitable. In order to curtail the possibility of having only abandoned infrastructure in the end, one has to think from the other side of the devastation. Infra Net Lab/Lateral Office explains it in the language of promotional brochures:

"The Caspian Sea's oil rig field is retrofitted for post-oil occupation by wildlife, maverick entrepreneurs, and adventure seekers."[6]

Resource depletion, even if still *in potentia*, establishes "retrospectively," from a future that can't be imagined any other way, the horizon of possibility for current design. Inexistent, projected, the deserts to come are the regulative force that determines what will be produced. An architectural need is formulated in such a way that any call to curtail the progress of destruction is rendered beside-the-point and romantic. This is the new normal, the way that power is extracted from the only future that transnational capital proposes as conducive to its maintenance and growth. Like credit in the financial sphere, pre-emptive design objectifies the future before it even arrives. Pre-emptive design capitulates to an erosion of critical distance in order to vindicate itself as the pragmatic-ethical option: it is willing to look the bitter truth in the face and devise, in an unsentimental way, the best possible solutions for the depredation that is coming. It doesn't look ahead in order to imagine detours, to insert counterfactual possibilities. Rather, it stares down that romantic option and soberly and pragmatically accepts that the only agency possible is that of the hard-boiled social clairvoyant: she knows what's coming so the best she can do is hide tents and rafts and bottles of water in the houses that the hurricane will devastate. This is just a step removed from "the superstitious compulsion to make some gesture when we are observing a process over which we have no real influence."[7]

———

When we speak of 'post-Fordism,' 'immaterial labor,' 'cognitive capitalism,' 'precarity,' etc. , we are certainly speaking of the material conditions and effects of capitalism as it currently functions. However, these are its conditions as it explicitly relates *to us*. This is what materializes on the side of current capitalism that interfaces with the human. What if we attempt to take stock of it from a different vantage point? What if we read capitalism not how in it manifests itself in relation to human bodies but in relation to what its *destination* reveals it to be: an Alien monstrosity, an insatiable Thing, that appropriates the energy of everything it touches and, in the process, propels things toward the inorganic? After all, aren't depletion and dissolution its underlying logics? aren't they what accompany its rampant drive to growth, its myth of unending prosperity?

Isn't it consistently and egregiously dragging things—natural resources, ways of life, communal values, traditional forms of social organization, symbolic systems, laboring bodies, public spheres, social safety nets, self-sufficient economies, entire populations (animal and human), the destabilizing potential of formal innovation in aesthetic production, even happiness—to their terminus, either to complete annihilation or to subsumption under a logic of general equivalence? What if we propose that capitalism has something like agency and that this agency is manifested in ecophagic material practices? Capitalism eats the world. Whatever transformations it generates are just stages in its monstrous digestive process.

Surely this is what someone like Nick Land has in mind when he proposes that "the history of capitalism is an invasion from the future by an artificial intelligent space that must assemble itself entirely from the enemy's resources."[8] It feeds on what it finds, leaving behind a metaphorical grey chemical sludge. This alien intelligence from the future seems committed to bringing about an ultimate inorganic state, the apocalypse of that final drag of everything into the post-biological, and it is working incrementally as it moves forward through history in order to realize the future it left "behind." Like a swarm of replibots run amok, capitalism feeds on this world in order to swell itself, but maybe not to swell into anything more than an enlarged, raging version of itself—like a massive hurricane, all de-personalized spinning forces looking to avoid any shoreline (political and economic alternatives) that may serve as a counterforce, chasing, instead, the conditions that will allow it to speed up and grow even more, to synthesize ever larger and more autonomous and automated assemblages. Its logic is embodied only in the swelling and the surging, in the effort to generate and maintain the conditions that accommodate and exacerbate this swelling and surging, which means, on an everyday level, parading as commonsensical the impossible idea of infinite economic growth. This may be the wavelength that Alex Williams is on when he proposes that

> what is necessary is to think the in-itself of capitalism outside of any correlation to the human...For surely what all analyses of capitalism have presumed to date is the capitalist 'for-us' (construed in positive or negative terms), whereas capital is ultimately a machine which has almost no relation to humanity whatsoever, it intersects with us, it has us as moving parts, but it ultimately is

not of or for-us. Capital properly thought is a vast inhuman form, a genuinely alien life form (in that it is entirely non-organic) of which we know all-too-little. A new investigation of this form must proceed precisely as an anti-anthropomorphic cartography, a study in alien finance, a *Xenoeconomics*... Marx's labour theory of value fails to think the capitalist in-itself, the ability to create value ex nihilo (i.e- credit, and all financial instruments constructed from variations on this theme). For Marx credit, 'virtual capital' and speculation built upon it is 'the highest form of madness'. Instead we ought to think of credit-based 'virtual' capital as the highest form of capital. This is not a mere semantic shift, but rather a revolutionary inversion of the L[abor] T[heory of] V[alue], following Deleuze & Guattari in considering capitalism-as-process, conducted upon pre-existing social forms, disassembling and reassembling them to suit its own nefarious and presently obscure ends. As process rather than concrete 'thing' we must consider its true nature to be contained in its destination, rather than the primitive building blocks from which it originally constituted itself (i.e- in the worlds of 'virtual' capital rather than the alienation of human labour, which is surely merely an initial staging post).[9]

Granted some license, we can graft the slimed and dead world that the "Grey Goo problem" promises to an imaginary point at which capitalism has realized the goal inherent to its compulsion to deplete. *It's the look of its destination*. As it's always the case with allegory, it's not that one scene replicates another, but that it recodes it in order to cast it in high-relief through imperfect but suggestive correspondences. One scene becomes a figural machine through which another one can be explained or approximated, particularly where direct representation is found wanting and the stiff edges of verisimilitude prohibit accurate depiction.

Seeing as the ground has shifted beneath current cultural production, a question to consider may be: What new options appear on the horizon for it by opening an "inhuman" perspective on this grey-goo capitalism? How do we do more than find the best compromise for a dissipative tendency that forcefully encodes itself in cultural objects, that works from the get-go to confiscate and annul divergent options to the kind of aesthetic artifacts that reinforce its naturalization?

Surely, there is the possibility of generating resistance, of finding new ways to counter the compulsion to expand at any cost, of articulating and producing or prefiguring new ways of living that challenge it. In short, there is the possibility of refusing any perspective that too quickly puts us under erasure, that disregards *a priori* whatever participatory, resistant, transformational, insurrectionary, and emancipatory gestures we may still muster. It may precipitous to disregard at this point what we may be able to accomplish, the ways in which we can still locate sites in which to intervene politically and where we can generate economic difference that interferes with and challenges the logic and kinds of relations that capitalism allows. We can still render visible practices that are currently discounted or repressed. This is, for the most part, what politically infused cultural projects, when smart, valiantly attempt, what still marks them as relevant in a lifeworld nowhere free of the tendency to absolute commodification and ruthless co-optation.

But just as surely we have to admit that there is a sense that the space for these politically infused and resistant projects is shrinking. The reach of their effects is increasingly localized and contained, when not just neutralized altogether, through different strategies, not the least nefarious of them being institutional appropriation in the guise self-reflexive and critical practice. And, in the end, it's as much a question of institutional practices as it is of the very structure of the very institutions--namely, museums, alternative spaces, biennials, competitions, etc.--which most often serve as the platforms for politically-inflected cultural projects.

Not long ago, Franco Berardi wrote about one of the continuities between modernity and what has followed it: the idea of acceleration as an underlying principle. He proposes that, despite whatever changes characterize the social transition out of modernity, the drive to speed things up has survived the shift from the manufacturing sphere to the semiotic one. These days, "when the main tool for production ceases to be material labor and becomes cognitive labor, acceleration enters another phase, another dimension, because an increase in semiocapitalist productivity comes essentially from the acceleration of the info-sphere—the environment from which information arrives in your brain."[10] As is always the case with Berardi, he is interested in how these things function in relation to the human body. His metric is always anthropocentric. He finds a crisis point where the production of semiotic goods simply exceeds, in speed of production and management of quantity, the capacity for attention that the human brain can generate. It is, for him, a question of processing time for the brain—or, rather, of the lack of this necessary time and the general, free-flowing injunction that follows this shortage and seeps into production (cultural and entertainment-based) to make things increasingly easier for us. Everything must be easier, less meaningful, so that we can take in more of it, sacrificing robust experiences to mere informational ingestion. "More and more signs buy less and less meaning" as "our relationship to the world... become[s] purely functional, operational—probably faster, but precarious."

Berardi's suggested resistance to this is to call for a reactivation of the relationship of language to desire, to put the body back in the circulation of signs as a way to ground this circulation again, to make it sensuous, to reign it in so that it functions within the time constraints that the brain imposes. But what of a different tactic, one that is the very opposite of this and that may allow us to approximate things from a perspective unfettered from the human body as ultimate metric: an aesthetics that pivots on testing acceleration, on speeding things up even further, on disintegrating things more ruthlessly? If we tap capitalism's dissipative compulsion as a force to be deliberately folded back into our practices, does it have anything to offer? Can we draw unexpected morphologies and affects by intensifying this will to deplete? Can we push until mutations imminent to the recurring processes through which it perpetuates itself become manifest? Can we force random glitches in the patterns of reproduction? Can we speed up until the very notion of "making it easier" is no longer feasible, a kind of kaleidoscopic and liquid complexity spinning at desperate velocities foreclosing on it? Can we cease looking at the institution as an imperfect platform for critique and historical reflection, which it of course no longer is? Can we embrace the inorganic as a way to crack open pockets of resistance to it, to perturb our implacable movement toward it, to discover unexpected potentialities?[11]

[1] Wark, McKenzie, "An Inhuman Fiction of Forces" in Leper Creativity, p. 39, Punctum Books, 2012. PDF: http://punctumbooks.com/wp-content/downloads/Leper_Creativity_CYCLONOPEDIA_Symposium.pdf
[2] Drexler, K. Eric, Engines of Creation: The Coming Era of Nanotechnology, New York, Anchor Press, 1986, p. 172
[3] Freitas Jr., Robert A., "The Grey Goo Problem,"

Excerpted version of article "Some Limits to Global Ecophagy by Biovorous Nanoreplicators, with Public Policy Recommendations" (originally 2000) published on on KurzweilAI.net March 20, 2001, http://www.kurzweilai.net/the-gray-goo-problem#r2

[4] Freitas Jr., Robert A., "The Grey Goo Problem"

[5] Projects were collected in Infanet Lab/Lateral Office, Coupling: Strategies for Infrastructural Opportunism, New York, Princeton Architectural Press, 2011

[6] Infanet Lab/Lateral Office, Coupling: Strategies for Infrastructural Opportunism, p. 33

[7] Zizek, Slavoj, First as Tragedy, Then as Farce, London and New York, Verso, 2009, p. 11

[8] Land, Nick, "Machinic Desire," Textual Practice, Vol. 7 No. 3, 1993, p. 479

[9] Williams, Alex, "Xenoeconomics and Capital Unbound," Splintering Bone Ashes, 2008, http://splinteringboneashes.blogspot.com/2008/10/xeno-economics-and-capital-unbound.html

[10] Berardi, Franco, "Time, Acceleration, and Violence," e-flux journal, #27, September, 2011, http://www.e-flux.com/journal/time-acceleration-and-violence/

[11] Or: are these questions mere manifestations of our naivete, ways of duping ourselves into participating in a fantasy or a symptom generated by a dissipative compulsion that advances regardless of how we position ourselves in relation to it? Are we surrendering more than we mean to when we take this treacherous path? Are these questions blindly

groping for a kind of fetish aesthetics that allow us to have our transnational capitalism while claiming to be able to challenge it—to recover critical distance—from the inside? In other words, are they part of the general logic of our "post-ideologic" moment: a way to be radical at the level of the proposal, while acting in ways that help entrench and naturalize the structural necessities of the system at every other level? One should tread cautiously here.

The Grammar of Neoliberalism

Benjamin Noys

The God that Failed

Nietzsche famously remarked that 'I am afraid we are not getting rid of God because we still have faith in grammar...' [1]. While the on-going global financial crisis indicates that capitalism is now the 'God that failed', what concerns me is that we still have faith in the grammar. To be more precise, I want to suggest that our critiques of capitalism, and especially capitalism in its neoliberal form, may unwittingly replicate and reinforce certain elements of neoliberalism as a form of governmental rationality. In particular here I will be focusing on the political (or anti-political) form of what I call 'accelerationism': a mode which deliberately suggests the exacerbation and acceleration of capitalist forms as the means to break the horizon of capital [2]. I would add, however, that the criticisms I raise will also apply to other forms of contemporary radicalism that tend to posit some immanent or exterior 'force' intrinsically resistant to capital, whether that be Life, emergent complexity, enclaves, or lines of flight (to choose some common examples). What I want to suggest is that we need a better grasp of what this 'grammar' of neoliberalism (and of capitalism) might be, and how it might inflect and compromise our forms of dissent.

To be clear from the beginning, my aim is not to tell another story about an all-powerful and all-recuperating capital, which pre-empts, neutralizes, and redeploys all the tools of critique. This has become a common story in contemporary activism, fuelling a desire for radical separation or exodus from the forms of capitalist power [3]. The irony is that such a story sets up an opposition between the lines of flight, exodus, the powers of Life, etc. , on the one hand, and capitalism as vampiric Other or transcendent form of Empire, on the other. It is this opposition, this separation, which in fact produces an oscillation between the manic insistence on the powers of Life and the depressed lamentation at the recuperative powers of capital. Instead, I argue, it is only by understanding the more subtle ways in which our lives and experiences are mediated by capital that we can hope to negate and resist capital as a mode of dominance. The recognition of capitalism as an antagonistic and contradic-tory totality is more useful to chart resistance than a perpetual stand-off between the immanent powers of the multitude and the transcendent forms capitalist capture.

This is certainly an act of critique, primarily directed to pointing out the replication of the tenets of neoliberalism by those claiming to exceed or flee from it. That said, it does not claim simple immunity or position of moral superiority; this, I think, is a result of one of the truths of Marxism, which is not, as Fredric Jameson constantly points out, a *moral* critique, but rather a critique that begins from the actual and real contradictions, antagonisms, and tensions of the existing social forms, which is to say *capitalist* forms. In fact, as Jameson notes, a moral critique all too often stands in for Marxist critique, in the reactionary form diagnosed by Nietzsche as a mechanism of value-positing, hierarchisation, and generator of a (bad) *ressentiment*. [4] Many of the versions of contemporary theory and activism operate within the frame of the moral or the ethical, if not the quasi-theological, in their positing of a singular power of Life, or some other originary force of resistance, against all the forms of Power. In contrast, my aim is to explore a *political* critique, which is neither a counsel of elation nor of despair.

The Genealogy of Neoliberalism

To begin I want to return to a more precise description of neoliberalism as a form of governmentality through the prescient lectures Foucault devoted to this topic from 1978–1979. Misleadingly titled *The Birth of Biopolitics*, they might better be named *The Birth of Neoliberalism*. Foucault focuses on two sites of the emergence of neo-liberalism: Germany, first in the 1920s and 1930s, and then at the center of post-World War II German policy, and American anarcho-capitalism. What Foucault stresses is the novelty of neoliberalism compared to classical liberalism. Whereas classical liberalism tried to restrict the state's interference to open up a space for the market, under the schema of *laissez-faire*, neoliberalism operates a re-organization of the state itself which is superimposed by the market. The aim of neoliberalism is, in Foucault's words, 'a state under the supervision of the market rather than a market supervised by the state.' [5]

It was the extinction of the Nazi state that made post-war West Germany the ideal site to re-found the state in terms of the economic, in which legitimation was achieved through economic growth rather than in political terms. This economic legitimation could be posed against the 'totalitarian' past of Nazism and the 'totalitarian' present of the East German communist regime. For this reason neoliberalism operated through and solidified a 'state-phobia', by arguing that the tendency of any intervention to a state-controlled economy, planning, and economic interventionism would lead to totalitarianism – whether of 'left' or 'right'. In a provocative series of formulations Foucault argues that this 'state phobia' permeates modern thought, aligning the critique of the spectacle (Debord) and 'one-dimensionality' (Marcuse) with Werner Sombart's proto-Nazi critiques of capitalism [6]. Here we might say we can see the emergence of the 'grammar' argument, in the sense of a common phobia of the state that leaves us vulnerable to historical re-inscription under the terms of neoliberalism, or, as Foucault puts it:

> All those who share in the great state phobia should know that they are following the direction of the wind and that in fact, for years and years, an effective reduction of the state has been on the way, a reduction of both the growth of state control and of a 'statifying' and 'statified' governmentality. [7]

Therefore, an intrinsic anti-statism is not sufficient to distinguish a political program from the forms of neoliberalism.

What is the precise nature, then, of neoliberalism? Of course, the obvious objection to the 'anti-state' vision of neo-liberalism is that neoliberalism itself is a continual form of state intervention, usually summarized in the phrase 'socialism for the rich, capitalism for the poor'. Foucault notes that neoliberalism concedes this: 'neo-liberal government intervention is no less dense, frequent, active, and continuous than in any other system.' [8] The difference, however, is the *point* of application. It intervenes on society 'so that competitive mechanisms can play a regulatory role at every moment and every point in society and by intervening in this way its objective will become possible, that is to say, a general regulation of society by the market.' [9] Therefore, we miss the point if we simply leave a critique of neoliberalism at the point of saying 'neoliberalism is as statist as other governmental forms'. Instead, the necessity is to analyze how neoliberalism creates a new form of governmentality in which the state performs a different function: permeating society to subject it to the economic.

According to Foucault, the forms of state intervention practiced by neoliberalism have some precise philosophical roots. First, this state intervention is *Kantian*; in that it is designed to act on the *conditions* of the social to create the possibility of competition and enterprise. It is important here to note that neoliberalism is opposed to the specter of the passive consumer just as much as various forms of leftism and anarchism, instead it wants to bring forth the person of enterprise and production. Secondly, Foucault traces the roots of German neoliberalism in the followers of Husserl. In this case competition does not emerge 'naturally', but only as an essence that has to be constructed and formalized: neoliberalism is *Husserlian*. Unlike in classical liberalism, we cannot 'free' market from the state and expect competition to emerge 'naturally'. Instead, the state constantly intervenes to construct competition at all levels, so that the market economy is the 'general index' for all governmental action [10]. These philosophical roots allow us to grasp the level of intervention of neoliberalism in a more precise way.

Foucault suggests that neoliberalism can be summarized in the program set out by the German economist Wilhelm Röpke in 1950, which proposes the objectives of government as allowing access to private property; reducing urban sprawl, which is to be replaced with private housing; the development of craft and small enterprises (described by Röpke as 'non-proletarian'); and the organic reconstruction of society on the basis of community, family, and the local. Foucault says: 'You will recognize this text; it has been repeated 25,000 times for the last 25 years.' [11] We could add it is being repeated now as well in the UK, as the 'big society' promoted by David Cameron's Conservative Party. At the heart of this vision, which is what makes it neoliberal, is 'this multiplication of the "enterprise" form within the social body and is what is at stake in neo-liberal policy. It is a matter of making the market, competition, and so the enterprise, into what could be called the formative power of society.' [12]

Foucault's point, which is germane to my analysis, is that critics of 'standardizing, mass society of consumption and spectacle, etcetera, are mistaken when they think they are criticizing the current objective of government policy.' [13] Neoliberal governmentality is not Keynesian and contemporary society 'is not orientated towards the commodity and the uniformity of the commodity, but towards the multiplicity and differentiation of enterprises.' [14] We can then group together this series of forms to note that neoliberalism poses a mode of intervention that profoundly reshapes social forms by acting on the conditions, especially the legal conditions, under which society operates, and which pays no heed to the 'naturalness' of markets forms, but rather treats them as something to be constructed.

What we need to register is that the neoliberal form of capitalism, which is of course not its only form or even its 'pure' form, operates in a way that includes and embodies critiques of the state, Keynesianism, and the 'Fordist' compact. Therefore, anti-statist radicalism—the drive beyond the state, the formation of alternatives to the state, and the search for anti-state enclaves—is closer than it imagines to neoliberalism as a form of critique. The delimitation of the power of the state and the power of the 'social' (as in social provision) is the aim of neoliberalism, along with the 'freeing' of an autonomous and local activity that is explicitly centrifugal. The emphasis on the complex, the organic, the multiple, and the differential, indicates that we are not dealing with the same 'grammar' as Keynesian social democracy. While I am not suggesting the simple equation of contemporary radicalism with neoliberalism, I am suggesting a more tangled series of convergences. The point here is the common departure and critique of social democracy. We might note this tense convergence in the shared slogan of 'No Future' that crosses between the punk moment of 1977 and the discourse of neo-liberalism.

Accelerationism=Neo-liberalism

To return then to the subject of 'acceleration-ism', which is a term which I coined as a means of identification and critique, but which has often been adopted in a valorizing fashion, I want to note how closely it conforms to these elements of neoliberalism. It incarnates a 'state phobia', it agrees with the necessity to subject all elements of society to the market, and it promulgates a vision of the 'person' as a multiple and differentiated 'enterprise' (in fact, we could note also Foucault's quasi-ironic, presumably, recourse to the language of the Deleuzoguattarian 'machinic' in his lectures). At least it would be hard to read this statement by Nick Land in any other fashion:

> Machinic revolution must therefore go in the opposite direction to socialistic regulation; pressing towards ever more uninhibited marketization of the processes that are tearing down the social field, 'still further' with 'the movement of the market, of decoding and deterritorialization' and 'one can never go far enough in the direction of deterritorialization: you haven't seen anything yet'. [15]

Land, quoting Deleuze and Guattari's *Anti-Oedipus* [16], appropriately goes further in making explicit the anti-socialist and anti-planning implications of their argument. Accelerationism, which it might willing concede, in this instance fully goes with the tide of the present.

The implication is that, in the language of Marx, this acceleration of neoliberalism will lead to a point of incompatibility with the capitalist integument, which will then be burst asunder. If capital is the barrier to its own development, as Deleuze and Guattari note by referencing Marx, then capitalism can only push beyond its own boundary through radical deterritorialization. [17][18] This deterritorialization is often coded by the presumption that the market is fundamentally incompatible with capitalism, contrary to our usual image. To make this assertion Land, and others, draw on the work of the historian Fernand Braudel. Certainly, Braudel draws out the fact that markets cannot simply be collapsed into capitalism, but he stresses that the market is a local and face-to-face form that can resist the opaque and centralizing powers of capital [19]. In contrast, Land and contemporary accelerationists often stress the market as a dispersive and liquid form that shatters or liquefies the capitalist barrier. The aim is not to return to the face-to-face, but to accelerate beyond the human.

In so doing they also presume a fundamental incompatibility of technological forces, especially the cybernetic and neurobiological, with capitalism. These 'forces' are generated by capital, but are presumed to exceed it or, more specifically, to exceed the human 'support' required by capital. This valorization is predicated on the valorization of the market as the acephalic field that releases and fosters these forces. Of course, markets have pre-existed capitalism and could post-date it and, of course, there is no simply essential or necessary reason why cybernetic or neurobiological forces are 'capitalist', or could not be re-assembled (to use Nicole Pepperell's formulation) for socialism or communism. That said, it seems to me accelerationism, and the critical and theoretical resources it draws upon, fundamentally misunderstands neoliberalism, as a particular form of capitalist governmentality, and capitalism itself, as a social form, and so *reproduces* them (or their own idealized image).

The fundamental schema, which obviously also extends to people like Antonio Negri and others, is to suppose that capitalism, in the style of the young Marx, is fundamentally parasitic and, in the style of the late Marx, that it has penetrated through real subsumption into the very biological and physical substrates of humans and the earth. The antinomy is then that we oscillate between the appearance of capitalism as mere skin, or exteriority, that can be easily discarded, and sudden lurches to a conspiratorial thinking of capitalism as utterly dominant. In a sense, which betrays a debt to Marx, capitalism is presented as the sorcerer's apprentice that unleashes forces it cannot control, not in the figure of the proletariat, but within its own 'productive forces'. Once we have shucked-off this parasite we can get on with the business of fully inhabiting inhuman capitalist *jouissance*.

What this kind of argument radically underestimates is that the domination of capitalism operates through the value-form, which is not simply an 'external' parasite but rather the 'self-positing' of capitalism as real abstraction. Markets and productive forces are not neutral social forms taken-up by capital, but fundamentally subsumed and reworked by the operation of value. To resist this self-positing effect, these kinds of radicalism suppose that capitalism is 'merely' an external 'power' or, in Bruno Latour's formulation [20], as a 'formatting regime', that tries to act on and grab pre-existent ontological richness. This is not to argue against the formulation that capitalism is a constant 'pumping-out' of value, but it is to argue that the real or practical abstraction of the commodity, especially the commodity of labor, penetrates and shapes existence horizontally and vertically. The 'shaping' is antagonistic and contradictory, but these contradictions and antagonisms are not simply external to the form of value.

Of course, at the same time, accelerationism, in its Negrian or Landian forms, accepts this real subsumption, but merely to argue that capitalism has now released forces which it cannot control and which we can expropriate. The claim here is that forces that are radically integrated into capital can release themselves from the bonds of capital. The result is symmetrical to the claim that there are ontological, social, or natural forces that somehow escape capital from the beginning. Here, again, I think nothing is grasped of the *forms* of production, accumulation, and the market which shape these so-called 'productive forces' – forces, which Marx noted, are capitalist through-and-through: capital absorbs labor, transposes it into production, as a form or relation of production [21]. Also, in this valorization of production coded as ontological power, or power unleashed, nothing is grasped of the fundamental *stasis* of capitalism; how its accumulation is not fundamentally 'creative', but rather an 'inertial' drift [22]. Capitalism is *deflated* into mere integument, and *inflated* in its creative power.

In terms of the more precise context of neoliberalism what is not grasped, as I've already intimated, is the 'fit' or conformity between accelerationism and neoliberalism. The dimension of governmentality is missed; the market is treated as neutral social form, without any thought about its conditions, and the constant action on those conditions, that might be required *not* to reproduce capitalism. In this way the market becomes hymned as *the* social mechanism, with its 'blind idiocy' translated into an Azathothic immanence. The state also is regarded as an exterior parasite, without considering in any real way, as was long ago argued by Karl Polanyi [23], how it helped to create this 'market' form, which penetrated and shaped the commodification of money, land, and labor. The 'minimal state' is taken as a given and only retains interest as the harnesser of 'war machines', leading to a fetishisation of military ideology and technology. Finally, the 'enterprise' is valorized is the 'enterprise' of self-deconstruction or self-extinction, whether that is cast in neurological re-tooling, biological re-formatting, or cyberspatial redistribution: a bloated 'anti-Oedipus'.

We are expected, in the name of Deleuzoguattarian anti-fascisms, to embrace capitalism as nihilist machine that has no 'purpose', because 'purpose'=fascism, while forgetting that neoliberalism appeared in Germany as the form of governmentality that would immunize us against fascism by trading the political for the economic. We are expected to accept, and welcome, state intervention to shape social forms to the market while repeating the mantra 'No New Deal', because Keynesian social intervention is quasi-totalitarian, and will only reinforce a 'socialist' capitalism, while forgetting the birth of neoliberalism out of anti-Keynesianism. No 'putting on the brakes', of course, as we can only accelerate to the future.

Alarmingly, and counter-intuitively, the context of financial crisis has done nothing, seemingly, to alter the popularity of this schema [24][25]. Acceleration may be into the abyss, but acceleration must be maintained. Social abstractions may have become frozen into morbid and malignant forms, but they must be re-started by another round of hyper-creative destruction. What is at fault is not capitalism, but its impurities, in a repetition of the mantra of those one-time 'masters of the universe' turned temporary beggars for handouts. Accelerationism takes on the form of an unearned nostalgia for the very recent past – a capitalist *ostalgie* – or neo-Orientalist fantasies of Sino-capitalism, with unrestrained biotechnology and no Judeo-Christian hang-ups. Operating in the mode of a macho hard-edged realism, what accelerationism attests to is the poverty of a theoretical imagination unable to reconstruct any rationality in the present and is instead content to wallow in the fantasmatic residues of capitalism's own irrationalisms.

[1] Nietzsche, Friedrich, The Anti-Christ, Ecce Homo, Twilight of the Idols, and Other Writings, eds. A. Ridley and J. Norman, Cambridge, Cambridge University Press, 2005, p. 170

[2] Noys, Benjamin, The Persistence of the Negative: A Critique of Contemporary Continental Theory, Edinburgh, Edinburgh University Press, 2010, p. 5-9

[3] Q. Libet, Alicw Preoccupied: The Logic of Occupation, New York, 2009, http://libcom.org/library/preoccupied-logic-occupation

[4] Jameson, Fredric, The Political Unconscious, 1981, London, Routledge, 2002, p. 172–193

[5] Foucault, Michel, The Birth of Biopolitics: Lectures at the Collège de France, 1978-79, trans. G. Burchell, Basingstoke, Palgrave, 2008, p. 116

[6] Ibid., p. 113–4

[7] Ibid., p. 191–2

[8] Ibid., p. 145

[9] Ibid., p. 145

[10] Ibid., p. 121

[11] Ibid., p. 148

[12] Ibid., p. 148

[13] Ibid., p. 149

[14] Ibid., p. 149

[15] Land, Nick, "Machinic Desire", Textual Practice 7.3, 1993, 471-482., p. 480

[16] Deleuze, Gilles and Felix Guattari, Anti-Oedipus, 1972, trans. M. Seem et al, London, Continuum, 2004, p. 260

[17] Ibid., p. 251

[18] Marx, Karl, Capital Vol. III, Marxists Internet Archive, 1996, http://www.marxists.org/archive/marx/works/1894-c3/ch15.htm.

[19] Wallerstein, Immanuel, "Braudel on Capitalism, or Everything Upside Down", The Journal of Modern History 63.2, 1991, p. 354–361

[20] Latour, Bruno, Reassembling the Social: An Introduction to Actor-Network Theory, Oxford, Oxford University Press, 2005

[21] Marx, Karl, Grundrisse, trans. Martin Nicolaus. London, Penguin, 1973, p. 308-309

[22] Balakrishnan, G., "Speculations on the Stationary

State", New Left Review 59, 2009, p. 5-26

[23] Polanyi, Karl, The Great Transformation, 1944, Boston, Beacon Press, 1957

[24] Srnicek, Nick, "The Accelerationist Critique of Neoliberalism", 2010, http://lse.academia.edu/NickSrnicek/Talks/24657/The_Accelerationist_Critique_of_Neoliberalism

[25] Williams, Alex, "Xenoeconomics and Capital Unbound", Splintering Bone Ashes blog, Sunday 19 October 2008, http://splinteringboneashes.blogspot.com/2008/10/xenoeconomics-and-capital-unbound.html

Death as a Perversion: Openness and Germinal Death

Reza Negarestani

A shattered introduction.

From pre-Islamic Zoroastrian mages to Sade to Nietzsche, Bataille and Deleuze, the investigations into openness have been always accompanied by at least five supplements: life, death, horror, outside and intensity. Openness has been diagrammed as both a tactical line and strategy traversing these five supplements while crushing the dimensions between them. The desire for openness has been considered the desire for life, death, horror, outside and intensity and this is why it has been cautiously appropriated whether through desire itself or despotic rigidities. However, it has been never totally blocked, for even in the case of monolithic despotism and rigidity, we do not encounter closure but strictly economical openness which is the indispensable part of any paranoiacally isolationist organization. On the other side of this panorama (economical openness), the survivalist approaches (economic, political, social, etc.) to desire have been more creative in appropriation/domestication of openness; the desire for openness has been domesticated through complex economic networks through which openness is translated as affordance; a survivalist horizon distributing or at least trying to distribute communication through the networks, in which fluxes of desire are merely forming a complex web of transportation systems or a hydraulic economy which is dynamic and flowing but empowering solidity and its complex survivalist circulations by stirring and transporting them, or even assisting solidity to assemble its own sphere of pseudo-fluxes where solid is softened, becomes extremely dynamic, versatile and forming its free-play institutions as it moves (as in fluvial/alluvial processes). Through affordance, openness is represented as the level of being open (to) not being opened (the plane of epidemic and contagion: plagues, contaminations, possession, etc.). "I am open to you." means, I have the capacity to bear your investment or 'I afford you' (this is not an intentional conservative voice but what arises as the fundamental noise produced by the machinery of different levels of organization and boundary, and finally organic survival); if you exceed this capacity I will be cracked, lacerated and laid open.

The Zoroastrians were among the first people who discovered and experienced the lacerating nature of openness and its contagious (or rather to say, the contaminative) space, thirsty to lacerate dimensions, crushing borders, snuffing them out and unleashing its epidemics (as epidemic is an avatar of openness) which confound the lineaments of openness as 'being open'. Deleuze indirectly speaks about the dangers of desire for total openness. Erich Fromm's concern is to argue the severe dangers of undomesticated or total openness, as openness traverses death, life, outside and intensity simultaneously while bumping them into each other, opening the virulently toxic expanses before the survival and bio-ethical horizons, spreading a satanic intensity of life (which Fromm calls necrophilia, a pervert side of life itself or more precisely, its desiring space: philia) everywhere; as openness is the brutal and creative base-communication of life, a confluence of non-unitary lines of philia (desire and attracting bonds) which is interdimensional; as openness is imminent to life: giving rise to everything (even unlife) while anonymously coming from the compositional depths of life... but what lurks in the abysmal thirst for openness that makes it so dreaded? What is the shape (or specter) of the Thing unleashed by total openness?

Where is it? and such landscapes of epidemic, death, openness and desire dance under my skin:

To what extent can the openness of life be taken? Is such an openness possible? Is openness a subject of bio-philosophy? Does the Deleuzian project of epidemic (epidemic desire, epidemic becoming, becoming epidemic, etc.) which roots the understanding of philia (as a space of multiplying bonds: love, desire, attraction, communication, etc.) on the plane of immanence really engineer the lines of what Keith Ansell Pearson calls Germinal Life [1]? And finally where is death in this epidemic openness? Subsequently, does necrophilia belong to Oedipus as "a race for death" (Deleuze and Guattari)?

And the questions proliferate as an epidemic on the move:

Philia as epidemic.
The word 'death' has the same mix of referential richness and conceptual poverty as the sign lifting a speed restriction. It would designate a concept only if this semiotic transition were treated as the representation of absolute velocity, rather than an incitement to free-flow. Dying is the departure from a traffic system, but this emigration

is not transcendentally governed by a pure destination. [2]

Life is the sexual plateau of all fetishes; death is only a perversion on this plateau. [3]

Erich Fromm in *Die Seele des Menschen* warns about a satanic intensity of life storming the bio-ethical horizons of the human race; a Mistmare (an untraced and unreported plague) which is cryptogenic (Incognitum Hactenus: anonymous-until-now) yet rising from the twisted nether of life in which survival is partly a joke and partly an economical repression. It is necrophilia which Fromm paranoiacally and artlessly opposes to biophilia, represents it as the ultimate fantasy of masculinity boiling out from the docile greed for domination, ownership and monopolization dedicated to Oedipality and the regime of doom and destruction in particular; consequently, he mistakes necrophilia for necrocracy through his inflexible bio-morality which reduces all creative communications to the interactions imprisoned within the logic of negativity and polar discourses.

Necrophilia is the expanse of base-participation and anonymous entities of power, "interphyletic collisions" (Nick Land) [4] and border collapse through which death as a zero-becoming or the absolute silence of intensity becomes problematic. Necrophilia is an event (in the Deleuzian sense of this word) germinated through epidemic bonds or contamination(an imminent and inevitable communication which pushes the entities toward an upheaval of proliferating and multiplying becomings through each other) and not death. This betrayal (or profound disloyalty) of necrophilia to death is what the Zoroastrians of ancient Persia experienced and discovered, and then, they ciphered Vendidad (The Book of Law against Demons or Anti-Druj laws) with it: that necrophilia and its systems of decay and germinal contamination cannot be coordinated with the other necro-oriented horizons of death. Necrophilia is life feasting on death or a life-infested death, an unthinkable intensity of life (a dimensionality wreckage of events and entities) that as Fromm remarks (but tries to repress and elude it) is unendurable, a satanic plateau which the Zoroastrians call Druj-, it is the Mother of Abominations, of all contaminations (base-participations).

Necrophilia is not the necrocratic regime of Oedipus or Philosophy, one can only (re) mold its history by economically commu-

nicating through its racialized boneyards
(of the Dead Philosophers?), it is a philia, a
strategic wreckage of life smeared on death
to the point of wearing it out, messing it with
its wasteful bonds, the bonds of philia, the
epidemic bonds. [5]

Necrophilia suggests a germination process
including folding, composition, terminal
softening, proliferation, split, recomposi-
tion and eternal fluidification through the
unground of philia, a composition of philia,
as philia is the engineering space of life, it
is constituted of bonds and alliances by and
through which desiring machines rise and
inter-communicate, and finally engineer
compositions of all forms (such as necrophilia). One might warn about the filiative
and tendentious nature of philia in the
cosmogonic models as what suggested by
Empedocles' philosophy and the rest of uni-
tary approaches; but considering philia on
a non-transcendental level, philia is neither
possessing, nor possessable; it is only conta-
giously open because the very bonds (of love,
friendship, alliance, fondness, etc.) which
make it philia, not as a capacity of tenden-
cies but a space of bonds which are pestilen-
tially fond of (the very meaning philia) everything, engineering alliances, transmuting
every process and relationship into a per-

verse love-making (the common meaning of necrophilia is a distorted apparition of this process) and finally, giving rise to inter-connective compositions, for compositions as Nick Land suggests are unfocused com-plexities [6] which do not allow the tenden-cies to gain victory or conquer the composi-tion's complexity by the institutionalizing of economical relationships through composi-tion but affirm them as modes or transient instances of multiplicities imminent to the composition. In such a space (philia) noth-ing remains pure since tendencies which try to forge purities are all contaminated and infected; they are interconnected by each other. Philia, even concealed under all ap-propriated features of Greek tradition, is a space where desiring machines unground ri-gidities, storm borders and dimensions; and necrophilia is an event germinated through this space, an instance of 'border collapse' and a perverse love (an anonymous plague of energy, excess and multiplying bonds composed as a process of contagion) which does not fail to incite becomings wherever it goes (contagion commotion). Meeting, com-municating or touching the true pestilential bonds of Empedocles' philia or the conta-gious plateau of interphylum or epidemic openness [7], the resistance, any isolationist struggle, uncommunicative reaction or opposition to remain unchanged (unmutated) becomes impossible (but appreciated as a strategy intensifying the mess, the waste of the process and engineering the exorbitant). Through the expanse of philia, everything should participate and participation has no end, nor beginning, nor horizon, nor a certain objective of participation. Infested by the epidemic (contagious and wasteful) bonds of philia, openness is triggered on all levels of its communicative lines but more on the plane of "being opened" than "being open" or "being open to". This is an openness abolishing or messing up all trajectories of economical communication, autarky and insularism: everything is terminally and ruthlessly softened and opened; this is what happens for the *necro* in necrophilia. Philia is an infection not in the term of invasion but unavoidable attraction (epidemic bonds: symbiosis, base-communication, parasitism, contamination, alliance, etc.) Through this openness, philia debases whatever attaches to it whether as a supplementary or articulative attachment (as in necrophilia). Philia does not answer the quiddity-oriented questions or the interrogations around genesis (oversimplifying philia as a rooted genesis element); it is the 'where' not as a question but an unground; philia is the unground where events or entities undergo a descent without stoppage; where everything is contagious, epidemic, compositional and under an immense ungrounding process. Through philia space is experienced in its non-accommodating / non-dwelling openness, an openness free from affordance-based (J. J. Gibson) or economical appropriations.

Philia does not unite or totalize -- Empedocles as a philosopher of Survival Economy, the Greek Genesis Project and cosmogonic regimes try to ascribe unification to philia, as if even thinking on philia is a horror for survival economy, its denizens, cosmogonic institutions around genesis and the anthropomorphic thought -- it mazes and storms by its epidemic openness, subverting dimensions, scavenging them, composing and bumping them into each other, introducing collapse to them. To this extent, brought to this plateau of base-communication (philia), necro (of necrophilia) is all laid and stripped open, infested and messed up in the unheard-of base-participations in life and the contagious bonds of philia. Through the interphyletic wreckages of philia (necrophilia, . . .), transcendental and dissecting levels of analysis (whether holistic or partitioning), if not appearing impossible, become extremely dangerous; extraction (e.g. extracting necro as death or a mortification process from the interphyletic wreckage of necrophilia) submerges in the fathomless depths of epidemic philia that is equal to being attracted and infected, being drowned into this compositional abyss, contamination (being contaminated) or being laid open by the bonds of philia. Contamination delays the extraction process or any analysis on a transcendental level to no end. In necrophilia, the 'necro' strips open and takes an anonymous life under the epidemic bonds of a contagious openness (philia) infecting through the strategies of life. Attraction or more accurately, epidemic bond is the functioning of philia (or epidemic openness) or as Deleuze and Guattari remarked "attraction is the functioning itself" [8] but in such an openness (and its avatars such as necrophilia) attraction is a hunt in the strategic ways (It knows nothing of lack.), where, always, the hunt is on. The sepulchral affirmation in necrophilia is also a hunt for openness, an anti-survivalist approach to openness and communication: being laid open. Necrophilia is the ultimate of such dimensionality wreckage engineered by the multiplicities and proliferation of philia as a creative space and not a concept or a horizon of nature; it is a hunt multiplying on the pestilential bonds of philia and through the war-strategies of life; however, certain segments and instances of necrocracy and Oedipalizing webs may enter in and try to appropriate this virulent openness but they are just trapped, recomposed and softened to no end through the bonds of philia, they just strategically enrich the battlefield, the dimensionality wreckage of mess engineering. Infested by philia, death is not domesticated; it goes rabid.

Germinal Death or the Mistmare.

Such an epidemic plague infesting and totally anonymizing death is one of the main traces investigated by the contemporary Russian necrorealist cinema known as Chernukha (blackness), mainly founded by the directors such as Evgenii Iufit, the Aleynikov brothers, Boris Youkhananov, Debil Kondratiev, et al. A radical movement started in Leningrad mainly with an inclination primarily toward the underground counter-culture of the mid 80s in Russia. The desolated landscapes of economic meltdown, lack of horror cinema or a science-fictional future in the collapsing Soviet Union and the Post-Soviet era, intense strife between the necroeconomic terror of survival economy and horror of life, collapse of thermoeconomical markets, and finally, cold-melt process of the necrocratic institutions, all have composed a web of netting heterogeneities, unnatural, unlocalizable and chronologically discontemporized to all politico-economic terrors in recent decades or a dystopian future; in one word, rendering a chaotic geography so terminal that any occidental / oriental discontaminating cultural, economic or social solution has been proved both inapplicable and dangerous not for Russian anonymous labyrinths but for the Eastern and Western countries themselves. Encountered with such an ample pestilential opportunity, the Russian artists started to investigate how the necrocratic regimes rot and their power formations are ungrounded within the shell of institutions, architectonic solids and political survivals but in fact exterior to them; how solidity is not wiped out and sucked into Zero but necrotized and softened to no end, shatters on the virtual surfaces of Zero without being sucked by its vortices, making its own economicgrund, a (un)grund whose tectonic expansion is the Zero itself (p/o); and how masculinity does not take the voyage of becoming-woman as its space of becoming but bites itself, appearing as the extreme homophobic/erotic irony of the impossibility of any final deliverance one can anticipate as the satisfying end of masculinity; however, considering and charting all these not as the illustrations of life emptiness (a survivalist or absurdist approach) or mortification as a collective response to social disorders and the problem of subjectivity (a crisis-based reaction), but affirmation (acting as companion) of a non-survival-supporting life whose tentacles crack death open merely as a collective perversion, a philia, which progressively disterminalizes as the end of all becomings or the terminus ad quem of becomings; and is transmuted to a collapsing expanse exhumed, deflowered and scavenged by life (non-survivalist life: unlife), its netting, mazing and bonding philia: a space of becomings, so contagious and epidemic, which as Nick Land puts it, is a "Pest" [9], a "meltdown plague" [10] (similar to Chernobyl Chinese syndrome) which does not serve the fluxional faith of the flux (becoming as fluvius) or pseudo-theological becoming (an unconventionally reductionist and characteristic, Eigentümlichkeit, becoming that is pregnant of some kind of stealth negativity) which Catherine Malabou suspects about Deleuzian becoming [11], but a terminal multiplicity in the form of evaporation, a GAS-becoming where molecules do not play the role of constituting or designing agents of flux-movements any longer; they become the pestilential ungrounding forces, the surface-consuming plagues; whatever they do is ungrounding (exhumation: ex +

humus: ground), irreparable and undoable; each molecule becomes a miniature of amazing earthquake. Such evaporations (Gas-becomings) and ungrounding / anonymizing becomings do not depict a "pure insertion into the cycle of metamorphoses" [12] that rummages through the stealth circulations of pseudo-flux (where flow is appropriated by grund) to locate its temporary (transient) and dynamically appropriated Utopias (the stages or expressions of metamorphing process); for meta-morphosis expresses a movement which, temporarily and dynamically, is appropriated by the ground it traverses to generate a fully dynamic and somehow unlocalizable formation; a non-institutionalized movement but a messenger of grund, a movement forced to transport a formation (morphosis), to express the ground dynamically, to disseminate the regulations of ground like fluvial / alluvial processes, irrigation systems fertilizing the ground and hydraulic architectures (as the State war-machines) which Wittfogel investigated in his *Oriental Despotism: a Comparative Study of Total Power* (1963). In Chernukha, as through the anonymous and undomesticated horizon of Russia with its vertiginous simplicity (or as Sergei Medvedev suggests The North or The_ Blank_Space [13]), death as a terminal expanse of coldness and a part of desiring-machine is messed up through the pestilential and wasteful (exorbitant) bonds of epidemic life (philia) which frantically composes new strategies of 'openness to everything' -- by means of its ungrounding strategies, bonds of philia and affirmation -- not merely openness as the plane of being open but rather being lacerated, cracked, butchered and laid open ... then, sewing and scavenging what have been opened through the bonds of philia and the interphyletic labyrinths of life through which becoming runs as a vermiculating, mazing machine or an engineer of labyrinthine inter-dimensionalities. Once death is infected (and infested) by the true satanic horror of life and its opening / affirming strategies or epidemic bonds of philia -- triggered by the auto-collapse of all survival economies and necrocratic regimes -- opening and being opened gruesomely is inexorable; the exhumed and scavenged death is sewn together as the lines of a new becoming (anonymous-until-now) trapped in the interphyletic and pestilential bonds of philia and life; it becomes a germinal death or a becoming(s), disloyal to Zero. To call it germinal death is because it has a germinal intensity within itself; it has been infected and infested with a germinality which can only be diagramed and perceived through the inter-dimensionality and the fathomless epidemic of philia and its openness and not life alone since this germinality which death has been infected with is not the Deleuzian movement from an organized body to 'the body without organs', the vortex of zero or death, for death itself has been laid open (infected, contaminated and butchered) and disterminalized (brought to an ultimate openness) under the constant and progressive ungrounding processes unleashed by the desiring machines or the epidemic / plaguing agents of philia; this germinality is a total and dangerously epidemic Openness, it is not movement but pure openness (in the sense of epidemic), it does not move since it is an absolute ungrounding process of ground or a horizon which makes all lines of tactics (movements) and at the same time, their domestication possible (movements, fluxes or tactical lines can only run and flow in the presence of dimensions, surfaces and other attributes of grund [14]), an openness which infects and attracts, merely radiating openness, its war against closure is purely strategic and not tactical [15]which needs ground as its horizon. However, what makes this germinality germinal and not something else is that it is a space of becomings and heterogeneities giving rise to the new things (modes of power, entities, etc.) like the germinality that Deleuze diagrams;

however the lines of these ungrounded becomings (of this ungrounded germinality) do not envelope a becoming-death as their zero-intensity (extinguishable intensity) or final silence [16] any longer, for, once again, death has been disterminalized, infested and cracked open. Openness bites into death, chews and liquidates it by its enzymes.

Germinal death is death transmuted to a new becoming or rather a space of becomings through which death surpasses itself through a brutal opening process; death itself is disterminalized by transmuting to a becoming that is anonymous (and imperceptible) even to zero but not external to it. Death actually happens but merely as a collective perversion (an infested practice with its own anonymous and contaminated intensities) through the epidemic bonds and the interphyletic labyrinths of philia. This is why Russian psychoanalyst Victor Mazin considers Chernukha and necrorealism as the anonymous landscapes of "the mutual contamination of life and death" [17]; or as previously discussed, base-necrophilia. Where even death is infested, then, survival economy (and the necessity of surviving for the organic body) as the base-ground of necrocracy loses all its politico-economic conservatism, mutates into a virulent strategy augmenting the collapse of any stratification process on its holy ground, acts as a camouflaged ungrounding process: solidity becomes virulent and messy; institutions become deterritorializing machines (as in the Post-Soviet space). This is where necrophilia (Chernukha) unleashes itself as a brutal schizotrategy working at the heart of paranoia as an ungrounding force. Through germinal death, the survivalist subject or the avatar of solidity does not try to survive but to soften itself progressively, to become an avatar of the ultimate softness; however, it does not choose or follow the liquidation that flux or conventional destratification processes use to mollify solidity; it installs decay (what is supposed to be a characteristic process of the regime of doom and destruction and the Oedipus race as Deleuze warns) as its softening machine, as a way of replacing surviving with eternal decomposition and rotting processes not on the plane of paranoia but schizotrategy and anti-solidity. Decomposition and decay stop because of the limits that death (or the great void) draws; in germinal death, however, they progress and persist endlessly. Decay appears as a strategic anti-rigidity process working through paranoia, using a brutal and fanatic destratification which is utterly dangerous and somehow disloyal to both schizophrenia and paranoia; what it only cares about is delirial softening.

To this extent, desire for germinal death is not geminated on the great silence or the cosmic tides of entropy, but as Nick Land suggests, "Pest."

In a transcendental interrogation, if becoming-death is the zero-collapse of all becomings, then what is that Becoming which infects death, demonically possesses it, pervades and infiltrates it, and in a turbulent motion ungrounds death through the epidemic openness of life through which everything is scavenged as an interphyletic wreckage or a maze of the affirming bonds? What is the becoming-infected death (germinal death) which loses its terminality, crosses itself as a becoming and becomes anonymous even to Zero but not external to it, a death cracked open by the affirming strategies of the satanic chemistry of life which allows the survival economies to be grounded as part of mess engineering and its grand strategic design for universal ungrounding? Is it Anonymous-until-Now (incognitum hactenus)? Or a lie or as the ancient Zoroastrians called it, Druj-, the feminine blackening upheaval, a universal ungrounding force or the Mother of Abominations -- Druj- means lie or strategy, the Mother of Abominations (Mistmare) or the life-satan according to Vendidad or the Zoroastrian Anti-Druj Laws -- by whose ungrounding forces, survival is rendered a catastrophic blindness through the dark chemistry of life?

Chernobog, Chernobyl, Chernukha.

Call it Chernukha cinema, contemporary Russia, the Mistmare (Mother of Abominations) or germinal death; it ungrounds death to the point that it (death) cannot be charted on the logic and the plane of the Outside; and the Outside as a horizon which renders the outlines of our thoughts, politics and economies and finally horror loses its creative and significant existence. We come to an expanse of juxtaposed death (Non esse apud se) or a dimensional wreckage (a terminal intimacy as in demonic possession) in which death is extra-proximal, assuming a germinal process of its own through life. Death itself becomes a germinal unlife. In such a non-judgmental upheaval, death cannot serve the outside any longer or the other way around; horror leaves the Outside or Baudrillardian Double as its fungal oceans and becomes a cryptogenic process which rises everywhere that philia germinates. The Bataillean eye, the eye of the Outside, is turned inside out; becomes an evaporative eye. The cult of the Eye must be the cult of philia, the Mother of Abominations, Chernukha and the germinal death. Chernukha does not insinuate death as an outsider or the death-outsider as the principle of its horror but frenziedly tries to explore the space in which death is always beside one in a diabolic intimacy of zero-distance and multiplying closeness or more accurately the level of possession (possessing and being possessed: ungrounded), for possession (or demonic infestation) is always the closeness in the absence of measures, scales and judgments (metron), a molecular closeness. This extra-proximal death ('death-beside . . .') instead of the death-outsider has been disseminated as the imminent horror of a life whose necrocratic regimes and survival economies are progressively ungrounded, a life rabidly radiating its contagious lines, turning necrocracy to base-necrophilia, transmuting any communication to a strategic affirmation leading to a gruesome and inevitable openness (not 'being open to' as the liberalist and absolutely economical approach to openness but being lacerated, cracked and laid open).

The entities, the inter-dimensional entities of this germinal death have already swarmed our popular culture, horror genre, video games, literature, the internet and everyday life, triggered the rise of new cryptogenic (ungrounded) entities and networks of power, disloyal to any grounded(ing) approach or procedure.

Chernukha is not noir; it is a creative blackness inviting blindness as its only way of experience. It is beyond judgment.

[1] Pearson, Keith Ansell, Germinal Life: The difference and repetition of Deleuze, London & New York, Routledge, 1999

[2] Land, Nick, The Thirst for Annihilation: Georges Bataille and Virulent Nihilism, London & New York, Routledge, 1992, p. 174

[3] Negarestani, Reza, "Pestis Solidus: On the Economy of Pseudo-flux", 2002, http://www.cold-me.net/text/pestis.pdf

[4] Negarestani, Reza, "Conversation with Nick Land" in Homo.stasis: conversations, unpublished.

[5] Negarestani, Reza, "Pestis Solidus: On the Economy of Pseudo-flux"

[6] Land, Nick, The Thirst for Annihilation: Georges Bataille and Virulent Nihilism, London & New York, Routledge, 1992, p. 160-183

[7] For more details on the Epidemic Openness (being laid open rather than being open), Nietzsche and the strategy of affirmation see: Negarestani, Reza, A Good Meal and Cata, 2002, http://www.cold-me.net/

text/meal.html and http://www.cold-me.net/text/
cata.html

[8] Deleuze, Gilles and Félix Guattari, Anti-Oedipus:
Capitalism and Schizophrenia, trans. R. Hurley, M.
Seem, H. R. Lane, Minneapolis, University of Minne-
sota Press, 1983, p. 330

[9] Negarestani, Reza, "Conversation with Nick Land"
in Homo.stasis: conversations, unpublished.

[10] Ibid.

[11] See Malabou, Catherine, "Who's Afraid of Hegelian Wolves?", Deleuze: A Critical Reader, ed. Paul
Patton, Oxford & Massachusetts, Blackwell Publish-
ers, 1996, p. 114-138.

[12] Lyotard, Jean-François, Libidinal Economy, trans.
Iain Hamilton Grant, Indiana, Indiana University
Press, 1993, p. 210

[13] Sergei Medvedev, "The_Blank_Space: Glenn
Gould, Russia, Finland And The North", CTheory,
Online, 2000, http://www.ctheory.net/text_file?
pick=128

[14] 'f=p/a' suggests the linkage between tactical lines
and ground, where 'f' is flux, 'p' is power and 'a' is a
representation of surface.

[15] This germinality is of the contaminative and contagious potentialities and not destructive tendencies.

[16] On the death-enveloping machinery (part of
desiring machine) of every intensity Deleuze and
Guattari remark: "They control the unconscious
experience of death, insofar as death is what is felt in
every feeling, what never ceases and never finishes
happening in every becoming -- in the becoming-

another-sex, the becoming-god, the becoming-a-race, etc., forming zones of intensity on the body without organs. Every intensity controls within its own life the experience of death, and envelopes it. And it is doubtless the case that every intensity is extinguished at the end, that every becoming itself becomes a becoming-death! Death, then, does actually happen."
Deleuze, Gilles and Félix Guattari, Anti-Oedipus: Capitalism and Schizophrenia, p. 330
[17] Mazin, Viktor, "Excerpts from Cabinet of Necro-realism", Necrorealism: Contexts, History and Interpretations, trans. Maria Jett, ed. Seth Graham, Pittsburgh, Russian Film Symposium, 2001, p. 28-52

Oceanic Accelerationism

Ben Woodard

The environmental activist, conservation-
ist, and marine biologist Rachel Carson once
said that when life came ashore millions of
years ago it brought a piece of the ocean with
it. One of the strange constructive constraints of being on a land filled with things
was the eventual birth of trade and debt.
Economics, broadly construed (and schizo-
analytically eyed) threatens to, in a theory-
theoretical sense, speed us back to the sea
through a technological progress unbound in
the form of the capitalist accelerationism of
both. Under this metaphorical construction,
technology and capitalism broadly grasped
are those privileged fields that take us to a
world of pure fluidity, but is there a mad-
woman or madman of theory up to the task
of navigating these waters?

Many contemporary theorists (Sadie Plant,
Luciana Parisi, Nick Land) have soaked up
the 'flow frenzy' of a hyperbolic Deleuzianism, suggesting a material, and not merely
libidinal (a la Lyotard) saturation to the
solution. They embrace the call to run naked

into the world of theory and experiment like swimmers who have forgotten about the resistance of the water. Liquid capital—or financial capital—are the castle in the sand at the edge of the flood. Plant inhabits this territory in her push and pull between ultra fluidity and radical essentialism. Land, however, was more than aware of the threat of the oceanic. The desert as Body without Organs in Land is flooded by cyberfeminist oceans. He re-draws the Kantian schema as a rotting oil derrick in the face of a sublime tidal wave.

The signs of a flood are everywhere; a tsunami is how Carl Cederstrom and Peter Fleming begin their text *Dead Man Working*. [1] Drawing from a work by Franco Berardi, they describe a world in which the worker of post-Fordist capital inhabits an emotionally deadened waiting game, unsure of when and if the end of capital will come -- an end which may in fact coincide with the end of life. This uncertainty comes from a massive capitalist fluidity that crashes against locality. For financial capital, shaving milliseconds from trades also means the blasting of tunnels for fiber-optic cables linking city to city, a physical ungrounding of the land itself. The effects of capital have fully saturated not just the economic conditions, but also the very material conditions of life. It is not just a threat of precarity that we find ourselves under, but the possibility of expulsion from life itself.

Luciana Parisi describes how the materialization of the capitalist ocean have altered even the biological conditions of life. This arises in the effects the flows of capital has on the terms of the specific sexual exchanges of genetic material. She outlines Elaine Morgan's adaptation of Allister Hardy's theory of the aquatic ape, in which a shore-like existence leads to vaginal migration and the erasure of the visible and olfactory signs of sexual excitement. The tidal wave of capitalism washes away these biological signs in obscurity and re-codes them in cultural practices, practices that all too often result in a virulent sexism that simultaneously praises and rages against the fluidity of the feminine.

Yet, in *Zeroes and Ones* Sadie Plant ironically recasts this Edenic fall as a wave of possibility: we were once in a kind of oceanic happiness and then things went wrong, but how facetious is she being, since the fall she describes is now life itself? Capitalism is the form waiting for life; it is that which made possible exchanges beyond our own little ecologies. Plant convincingly demonstrates that the technological and material changes wrought by capitalism do not necessarily have to follow the restrictive ideals of a masculine ideology. Capital is the sufficient but not the necessary means of some fluidic regime, a regime which, if not in a panic with the associated sublime horror or monstrous feminine-- is simply the enemy of reason-- that which erodes the shores of rational discourse. One could argue that masculinized capital is a parasite on the potentialities of the feminine which then must deny and shore itself of any inherent (or non-obvious) teleology. But would a change to a more feminist ecological exchange threaten the nature of capitalism?

The exaggerated (maybe necessarily so?) move of the accelerationist is to hyperbolically/hyperstitionally enhance the spectral thing or system that is capitalism into a xeno-monstrosity, an alien that has been waiting for human hosts. [2] We (those human, all too human humans) seem torn between futilely swinging our swords at the incoming waves like mad berserkers rushing to our own drowning, or we seem committed to celebrating capitalism's destratification of all forces and all things. The revolutionary struggle has been miscast as a war against, and as a choice between, the apocalyptic costs of a masculanized capitalism, or a return to utopic pre-capitalist feminist ocean.

Are Deleuze and Guattari to blame? Do the hyperbole of accelerationism and cyberfeminism point to the rotting potato roots of their project? In 'Becoming Animal...' Deleuze and Guattari say: "So experiment." [3] But as Land points out in his stimulated analysis, this leads to an excess of tactics without strategy. [4] The problem is this: what capitalism seems to be doing—embracing all tactics to profit off of them—is accompanied by the necessity of applying a cost and this exposes an underlying strategy which is as obvious as it is gross: life itself is reduced to profit over cost. High speed trade and liquid assets have made an ocean out of capital and populated it with creatures (algorithms) which behave together in ways we fundamentally cannot predict (a firm unleashed alghorithms on its own company, managing to make it insolvent in less than a second). So if it is not even a jungle, but an ocean, and experimentation still requires breathing (underwater), then it is tempting to pollute. The trick of sustaining capital is that the costs incurred may be as or more expensive than its relatively positive creations. That is, the cost of experimentation is the affordability of allowing any given capitalist sea monster to expand its territory and keep swimming, without too much risk of drowning the whole enterprise.

What is required is a pollution that is mindful of the ecology of the whole, sea, including the life that dwells beneath, and not any one particular monster.

To be slightly less metaphorical, the ocean is calling: excess pollution (caused by excess consumption, excess buying, excess production) is melting the frozen parts of the world, filling things up with water. It becomes a game of all or nothing: life or capital? As Zizek has noted, it is harder to imagine a subtle shift in capitalism than it is to imagine the end of the world. The problem is, as has already mentioned, that capital absorbs the basic ecological logic of life (profit over cost, eat enough to keep existing) and expands the cost of existing to the cost of perpetuating capital, and to sustain an endless production which is, in itself, a material impossibility.

The accelerationism of capital does not merely mean intensifying it further, but opening it to the exorbitant outside that it has refused to absorb. It means making it less selective in its own internal assignment of cost when it refers to entities outside of it. It means engineering a permanent liquidity crisis. In a broad sense this is nothing particularly new to feminist critique, as it highlights the exclusion of particular cost in any exchange, an exclusion which has historically focused on women, on the contingent, the mad, the unpredictable, the amphibious maidens. Maybe this is why for Land the only proper revolutionary subjects are lesbian vampires.

Peter Watts in his Rifters series of Novels (*Starfish, Maelstrom, Behemoth and Behemoth Max*) documents a motley crew of individuals sent to watch over power stations on an ocean bottom rift, one of the last reliable sources of power on future earth. These people are strikingly posthuman, adapted biologically and technologically to work in their new environments and therefore chosen not for their scientific expertise but for the personality flaws that allow them to handle abuse and isolation.

In *Starfish*, the forces of capital are unable (albeit barely) to control the posthuman workers they have created. It is important to distinguish posthuman from posthumanist and transhuman. The posthumanist holds a stance in which we (whatever strange collective that designates) should move beyond the human in its humanist sense and foster deeper relations with our own components and the components of our wider ecologies (our pets, our plants, the other various creatures and inanimate powers, texts, and things which vibrate in our presence). Transhumans, following thinkers such as Ray Kurzweil, believe that the human can be technological or biotechnologically surpassed with one popular end goal being the achievement of the uploadability of all of human consciousness.

With the concept of the posthuman, both humanism and the human are moved away from, without a teleological bettering nor with the certainty that supposedly long held human characteristics will remain after a material shift in the human body. There is no clear sense of improvement, but a different kind of adaptation. The rifters eventually come to refer to themselves as vampires as they are emotionally cold creatures meant for working in the dark without empathy or desire to be amongst humans.

The vampiric, as Deleuze and Guattari explore in "Becoming Animal" through the widespread Vampire Hysteria of the early 1700s in Eastern Europe, is a particular form of becoming yet they do not address its noble lineage. While the zombie has become (starting with at least George Romero's films) the monster of capitalist disquiet, the vampire traditionally represents the lords of crumbling castles, of business people attempting to live out their retirement. As Marx puts it in the tenth chapter of *Capital*:

> Capital is dead labour, that, vampire-like, only lives by sucking living labour, and lives the more, the more labour it sucks. The time during which the labourer works, is the time during which the capitalist consumes the labour-power he has purchased of him.[5]

But Watts' vampires are the downtrodden worker. The trouble is that on the one hand, there seems to be no limits to the changes that capital writ large can incur in life—both life as everyday existence and life as actual biological existence. This is illustrated respectively by the increasing difficulty in getting 'out' of the office, and, as highlighted in hyperbolic terms by Watt's novels, with suicide seeds and copyrighted agricultural genomes. Yet there remain common barriers: one stressed by the limits of social connectivity and the other by material resources.

As the oceanic metaphor makes clear, being immersed in capital it becomes nearly impossible to diagnose our environment no matter how much economic friction remains. Economic crisis appears simultaneously too real and too abstract as either riots in the streets or as computational errors to be corrected by those officials with access and the capability.

How does one accelerate (in) a fluid medium?

Let's restate the problems:

1 - Technological capitalism (more than making all that is solid melt into air) makes solid or gives an extra layer of self-awareness to the creatures living in it. In this sense, capital becomes an ocean in which we swim, life seems unlivable without out and, the outlying bound of capital (which is the purely ideal impossible dream of limitless production) appears indistinguishable from the water at hand, from day to day life. Capitalism "has no external limit, it has consumed life and biological intelligence to create new life and a new plane of intelligence, vast beyond human anticipation."[6]

2 - Because of this illusion the cost involved in local exchanges is measured against not

only the local terms but against the far horizon of capital, while appearing ideally limitless is considered hyper-fragile in the intimacy of the exchange.

3 - This second issue is compounded by the history of practices of exogamy which demonstrate the simultaneous worth and worthlessness of women in patriarchal culture. Furthermore, the side of worthlessness can be equated with pure form or maybe even formlessness, that of the productive yet strangely undivided ocean.

4 - The ocean is populated with monsters... this is what Plant means with her something went wrong but that wrongness, that mistake is life itself. Or maybe the wrongness already registers once we achieve consciousness as Thomas Ligotti argues in *The Conspiracy Against the Human Race*. The violence between organisms may make it seem that capital is merely a more civilized way but it actually just expands the killing floor to the end of time. As Land writes: "Capital is not overdeveloped nature, but underdeveloped schizophrenia."[7]

5 - For all of these reasons the acceleration of capitalism seems impossible. The only possible options seem to be to drown or embrace

the catastrophe (and the catastrophe of the sea is the tidal wave, the tsunami). But it may very well be that the wave, as Cederstrom and Fleming put it, may never come.

One can watch the wave, as a sublime monstrosity in the properly Kantian way (thinking my schema will protect me) or hope that it will peter out and bring new playthings like it did for the children of Nietzsche's Zarathustra. But this assumes that the ocean will serve and not, eventually, absorb more and more of the sun in its darkened complexion (having lost its reflective ice) and will flood the shores.

It is that challenge which requires the separation of technological accelerants from capitalist ones. Land writes that Nature (a cold indifferent nature)[8] is not opposed to cybernetics but to the industrial.[9] Schizoanalysis, the strange pragmatics of an anti-molar deregulation of all existence is at once the expansive capacity of capital that it cannot disavow[10], as well as that which is capable of luring capital into liquidating its "fall back positions."[11]

Nick Land hits on a basic twofold thought for thinking the crux of capital and politics (a politics beyond that world being used descriptively in an academic setting). This is the gendering of both capital and politics in the territory of the active and the passive. Land writes:

> Wherever there is labour or struggle there is a repression of the raw creativity which is the atheological sense of matter and which - because of its anegoic effortlessness - seems identical with dying. Work, on the other hand, is an idealist principle used as a supplement or compensation for what matter cannot do. One only ever works against matter, which is why labour is able to replace violence in the Hegelian struggle for recognition. [12]

In November 1935 Bataille gave a speech at a gathering of Contre-Attaque called "Popular Front in the Street", in which he derided the overly parliamentary tactics of the Popular Front the synthesis of communists and socialists, that had recently taken over the street in France. Bataille's group Contre-Attaque set out to, in a sense, co-opt fascistic protocols and sharpen the teeth of the politics in France.[13]

Bataille says that he does not want to cause political change but calls for "a different nature."[14] Bataille ends his speech: "This All

powerful magnitude, thus human ocean...
only this ocean of men in revolt can save the
world from the nightmare of impotence and
carnage in which it sinks!' [15] The fluidity of
the ocean of workers is betrayed by Bataille's
own machismo—he does not know whether
he wants fluidity or solidity but is only sure
in his vaguely Nietzschean overtones.

Land gives us an excellent response:

> If feminist struggles have been constantly
> deprioritized in theory and practice it is
> surely because of their idealistic recoil from
> the currency of violence, which is to say,
> from the only 'definitive 'matter' of politics.
> [...]It is a terrible fact that atrocity is not the
> perversion, but the very motor of of such
> struggles: the language of inexorable politi-
> cal will. A revolutionary war against a mod-
> ern metropolitan state can only be fought in
> hell. [...] For it is only when the pervasive
> historical bond between masculinity and
> war is broken by effective feminist violence
> that it will become possible to envisage the
> uprooting of patriarchical endogamies that
> orchestrate the contemporary world order
> [...] we must foster new Amazons in our
> midst.[16]

An oceanic accelerationism, wired through

Plant and Luce Irigiray, is a marine violence, what Lennie Clarke, the anti-hero of Watts' tales learned by surviving domestic abuse, genetic manipulation, and attempted murder by a corporation.

To end on a strange aside: In the Marvel Comic universe there is a creature, an ancient self-aware bacterium from the oceanic depths, that possesses beings at will and sets out to erase all genetic mutations from the earth in order to be secure in its biologically rooted power. The name that this creature chooses for itself is sublime. This is the masculine impulse of capitalism personified, falsely positing itself as the transcendent sublime, in a brute attempt to deny the fluid mutations of the outside.

In one ridiculous gesture the weakness the ego in the face of nature becomes apparent (the Kantian schemata splitting the horrific from the sublime). The material vibrancy of the ocean will have the final judgment as long as we are complacent everywhere churlish masculinity is not. We must see capital as a great invention through which we can actively navigate uncertain waters, rather than as a sea monster, different from our own life only in its artificial provenance. Send out the distress call for cyberfeminism.

[1] See Cederstrom, Carl and Flemming, Peter, Dead Man Working, London, Zer0, 2012

[2] See Thacker, Eugene. "Oil Discovers Humans", in Leper Creativity, New York, Punctum, 2011

[3] Deleuze, Gilles, and Felix Guattari, "Becoming Animal...", A Thousand Plateaus, Minneapolis, Minneosta University Press, 1990

[4] On this point see Brassier, Ray, "Introduction to Nick Land", http://moskvax.wordpress.com/2010/09/30/accelerationism-ray-brassier/

[5] Marx, Karl, Capital: A Critique of Political Economy, Modern Library Classics, New York, Random House, 1906, p. 257

[6] Land, Nick, "Transcendental Miserablism", Fanged Noumena: Collected Writings 1987-2007, eds. Brassier, Ray and Robin Mackay, London, Urbanomic, 2011, p. 626

[7] Land, Nick, "Circuitries", Fanged Noumena: Collected Writings 1987-2007, p. 313

[8] Land, Nick, "Making it with Death", Fanged Noumena: Collected Writings 1987-2007, p. 261

[9] Land, Nick, "Circuitries", p. 313-314

[10] Land, Nick, "Making it with Death", 2011, p. 265

[11] Ibid., 287

[12] Ibid. 278

[13] Stoekl, Allan, "Introduction", Visions of Excess: Selected Writings of George Bataille, Minneapolis, Minnesota University Press, 1995, xviii

[14] Bataille, George. "Popular Front in the Street", Visions of Excess: Selected Writings of George Bataille, Minneapolis, Minnesota University Press, 1995,

p. 161

[15] Ibid., p. 168

[16] Land, Nick, "Kant, Capital, and the Prohibition of Incest," Fanged Noumena: Collected Writings 1987-2007, p. 79-80

To the Political Ontologists

Christian Thorne

The political ontologists have their work cut out for them. Let's say you believe that the entire world is made out of fire: Your elms and alders are fed by the sky's titanic cinder; your belly is a combustion engine or metabolic furnace; your lungs draw in the pyric aether; the air that hugs the earth is a slow flame—a blanket of chafing-dish Sterno—shirring exposed bumpers and cast iron fences; water itself is a mingling of fire air with burning air. The cosmos is ablaze. The question is: How are you going to derive a political program from this insight, and in what conceivable sense could that program be a politics of fire? How, that is, are you going to get from your ontology to your political proposals? For if fire is not just a political good, but is in fact the very stuff of existence, the world's primal and universal substance, then it need be neither produced nor safeguarded. No merely human arrangement—no parliament, no international treaty, no tax policy—could dislodge it from its primacy. It will therefore no longer make sense to describe yourself as a *partisan* of fire, since you cannot be said to defend something that was never in danger, and you cannot be said to promote something that is everywhere already present. Your ontology, in other words, has already precluded the possibility that fire is a choice or that it is available only in certain political frameworks. This is the fate of all political ontologies: The philosophy of all-being ends up canceling the politics to which it is only superficially attached. Theology swallows its adjective.

The task, then, when reading the radical ontologists—the Spinozists, the Left Heideggerians, the speculative realists—is to figure out how they think they can get politics back into their systems; to determine by which particular awkwardness they will make room for politics amidst the spissitudes of being. In its structure, this problem repeats an old theological question, which the political ontologists have merely dressed in lay clothes—the question, that is, of whether we are needed by God or the gods. If you have given in to the pressure to subscribe to an ontology, then this is the first question you should ask: Whatever is at the center of your ontology—does it *need* you? Does Becoming need you? Is Being incomplete without you?

Has the cosmic fire deputized you? And if you decide that, no, the fire does not need you—if, that is, you resist the temptation to appoint yourself that astounding entity upon which even the Absolute depends—then you will have yourself already concluded that there is nothing exactly to be gained from getting your ontology right, and you will be free to think about other and more interesting things.

If, on the other hand, you are determined to ontologize, and determined additionally that your ontology yield a politics, there are, roughly speaking, three ways you can make this happen.

First, you could determine that even though fire is the primal stuff of the universe, it is nonetheless unevenly distributed across it; or that the cosmos's seemingly discrete objects embody fire to greater and lesser degrees. The heavy-gauge universalism of your ontology will prevent you from saying outright that water isn't fire, but you might conclude all the same that it isn't very good fire. This, in turn, would allow you to start drawing up league tables, the way that eighteenth-century vitalists, convinced on argued grounds that the whole world was alive, nonetheless distinguished between *vita maxima* and *vita minima*. And if you possess ontological rankings of this kind, you should be able to set some political priorities on their basis, finding ways to reward the objects (and people? and groups?) that carry their fiery qualities close to the surface, corona-like, and, equally, to punish those objects and people who burn but slowly and in secret. You might even decide that it is your vocation to help the world's minimally fiery things—trout ponds, shale—become more like its maximally fiery things—volcanoes, oil-drum barbecue pits. The pyro-Hegelian takes it upon himself to convert the world to fire one timber-framed building at a time.

Alternately—and herewith a second possibility—you can proclaim that the cosmos is made of fire, but then attribute to humanity an appalling power *not to know this*. "Power" is the important word here, since the worry would have to be that human ignorance on this point could become so profound that it would damage or dampen the world-flame itself. Perhaps you have concluded that fire is not like an ordinary object. We know in some approximate and unconsidered way what it is; we are around it every day, walking in its noontide light, enlisting it to pop our corn, conjuring it from our very pockets with a roll of the thumb or knuckly pivot. And yet we don't really *understand* the blaze; we certainly do not grasp its primacy or fathom the ways we are called upon to be its tenders. You might even have discovered that we are the only beings, the only guttering flames in a universe of flame, capable of defying the fire, proofing the world against it, rebuilding the burning earth in gypsum and asbestos, perversely retarding what we have been given to accelerate. This argument speaks clear misgivings about humanity; it doesn't trust us to keep the fire stoked; and to that extent it partakes of the anti-humanism that is all but obligatory among political ontologists. And yet it shares with humanism the latter's sense that human beings are singular, a species apart, the only beings in existence capable of living at odds with the cosmos, capable, that is, of some fundamental ontological misalignment, and this to a degree that could actually abrogate an ontology's most basic guarantees. From a rigorously anti-humanist perspective, this position could easily seem like a lapse—the residue of the very anthropocentrism that one is pledged to overcome—but it is in fact the most obvious opening for an anti-humanist politics, as opposed, say, to an anti-humanist credo, since you really only get a politics once the creedal guarantees have been lifted. If human beings are capable of forgetting the fire, someone will have to call to remind them. Someone, indeed, will have to ward off the ontological catastrophe—the impossible-but-somehow-still-really-happening nihilation of the fire—the Dousing.

That said, a non-catastrophic version of this last position is also possible, though its politics will be accordingly duller. Maybe duller is even a good thing. Such, at any rate, is the third pathway to a political ontology: You might consider arguments about being politically germane even if you don't think that humanity's metaphysical obtuseness can rend the very tissue of existence. You don't have to say that we are damaging the cosmic fire; it will be enough to say that we are our damaging ourselves, though having said that, you are going to have to stop trying to out-anti-humanize your fellows. Your position will now be that not knowing the truth about the fire-world deforms our policies; that if we mistake the cosmos for something other than flame, we are likely to attempt impossible feats—its cooling; its petrification—and will then grow resentful when these inevitably fail. You might, in the same vein, determine that there are entire institutions dedicated to broadcasting the false ontologies that underwrite such doomed projects, doctrines of air and doxologies of stone, and you might think it best if such institutions were dismantled. If it's politics we're talking about, you might even have plans for their dismantling. Even so, you will have concluded by this point that the problem is in its essentials one of belief—the problem is simply *that some people believe in water*—in which case, ontology isn't actually at issue, since nothing can *happen* ontologically; the fire will crackle on regardless of what we think of it, indifferent to our denials and our elemental philandering. You have thus gotten the politics you asked for, but only having in a certain sense bracketed the ontology or placed it beyond political review. And your political program will accordingly be rather modest: a new framework of conviction—a clarification—an illumination.

Still, even a modest politics sometimes shows its teeth. William Connolly, in a book published in 2011, says that the world-fire is burning hotter than it has ever burnt; the problem is, though, that some "territories … resist" the flame. What we don't want to miss is the basically militarized language of that claim: "resisting territories" suggests backwaters full of ontological rednecks; Protestant Austrian provinces; the Pyrenees under Napoleon; Anbar. Connolly's notion

is that these districts will need to be enlightened and perhaps even pacified, whereupon
political ontology outs itself as just another
program of philosophical modernization,
a mopping up operation, the People of the
Fire's concluding offensive against the
People of the Ice. *Don't fight it*, Connolly, in
this way, too, an irenicist, instructs the exis-
tentially retrograde. *Let it burn*.[1]

The all-important point, then, is that there
is absolutely no reason to get hung up on the
word "fire," in the sense that there is no more
sophisticated concept you can put in its place
that will make these problems go away: not
Being, not Becoming, not Contingency, not
Life, not Matter, not Living Matter. Go ahead:
Choose your ontological term or totem and
mad-lib it back into the last six paragraphs.
Nothing else about them will change.

―――――――

Anyone wanting to read Connolly's *World of
Becoming*, or Jane Bennett's *Vibrant Matter*,
its companion piece, now has some questions they can ask.[2] The two books share a
program:

• to survey theories of chaos, complexity;
to repeat the pronouncements of Belgian

chemists who declare the end of determin-
ism; and then to resurrect under the cover
of this new science a much older intellectual
program—a variously Aristotelian, Paracel-
sian, and hermetic strain in early modern
natural philosophy, which once posited and
will now posit again a living cosmos a-go-go
with active forces, a universe whose intricate
assemblages of self-organizing systems will
frustrate any attempt to reduce them back to
a few teachable formulas;

• or, indeed, to trade in "science" altogether
in favor of what used to be called "natural history," the very name of which strips
nature of its pretense to permanence and
pattern and nameable laws and finds instead
a universe existing wholly in time, as fully
exposed to contingency, mutation, and the
event as any human invention, with al-
ligators and river valleys and planets now
occupying the same ontological horizon as
two-field crop rotation and the Lombard
Leagues;

• to recklessly anthropomorphize this
historical cosmos, to the point where that
entirely humanist device, which everywhere
it looks sees only persons, tips over into its
opposite, as humanity begins divesting itself
of its specialness, giving away its privileges

and distinguishing features one by one, and so produces a cosmos full of more or less human things, active, volatile, underway—a universe enlivened and maybe even cartoonish, precisely animated, staffed by singing toasters and jitterbugging garden shears.

I wouldn't blame anyone for finding this last idea rather winning, though one problem should be noted right away, which is that Connolly, in particular, despite getting a lot of credit for bringing the findings of the natural sciences into political theory—and despite repeating in *A World of Becoming* his earlier admonition to radical philosophers for failing to keep up with neurobiology and chemistry and such—really only quotes science when it repeats the platitudes of the old humanities.[3] The biologist Stuart Kauffman has, Connolly notes, "identified real creativity" in the history of the cosmos or of nature. Other research has identified "degrees of real agency" in a "variety of natural-social processes." The last generation of neuroscience has helped specify the "complexity of experience," the lethal and Leavisite vagueness of which phrase should be enough to put us on our guard. It turns out that the people who will save the world are still the old aesthetes; it's just that their banalities can now borrow the authority of

Nobel Laureates (always, in Connolly, named as such). Of one scientific finding Connolly notes: "Mystics have known this for centuries, but the neuroscience evidence is nice to have too."[4] That will tell you pretty much everything you need to know about the role of science in the new vitalism, which is that it gets adduced only to ratify already held positions. This is interdisciplinarity as narcissistic mirror.

But we can grant Connolly his fake science—or rather, his fake deployment of real science. The position he and Bennett share—that the cosmos is full of living matter in a constant state of becoming—isn't wrong just because it's warmed over Ovid. What really needs explaining is just which problems the political philosophers think this neuro-metamorphism is going to solve. More to the point, one wonders which problems a vitalist considers still unsolved? If Bennett and Connolly are right, is there anything left for politics to *do*? Has Becoming bequeathed us any tasks? Won't Living Matter get by just fine without us? And if there is no political business yet to be undertaken, then in what conceivable sense is this a political philosophy and not an anti-political one?

The real dilemma is this: There are those

three options for getting a politics back into ontology—you can devise an ontological hierarchy; you can combat ontological *Vergessenheit*; or you can promote ontological enlightenment. Bennett and Connolly don't like two of these, and the third one—the one they opt for—ends up canceling the ontology they mean to advocate. I'll explain.

Option #1

Hierarchy could work. Bennett and Connolly could try to distinguish between more and less dynamic patches of the universe—or between more and less animate versions of matter—but they don't want to do that. The entire point of their philosophical program is a metaphysical leveling; witness that defense of anthropomorphism. Bennett, indeed, uses the word "hierarchical" only as an insult, the way that liberals and anarchists and post-structuralists have long been accustomed to doing. Having only just worked out that all of matter has the characteristics of life, she is not about to proclaim that some life forms are more important than others. Her thinking discloses a problem here, if only because it reminds one of how difficult it has been for the neo-vitalists to figure out when to propose hierarchies and when to level them, since each seems to come with political consequences that most readers will find unpalatable. Bennett herself worries that a philosophy of life might remove certain protections historically afforded humans and thus expose them to "unnecessary suffering." She positions herself as another trans- or post-humanist, but she doesn't want to give up on Kant and the never really enforced guarantees of a Kantian humanism; she thinks she can go over to Spinoza and Nietzsche and still arrive at a roughly Left-Kantian endpoint. "Vital materialism would … set up a kind of safety net for those humans who are now … routinely made to suffer."[5] That idea—which sounds rather like the Heidegger of the "Letter on Humanism"—is, of course, wrong. [6] Bennett is right to fret. A vitalist anti-humanism is indeed rather cavalier about persons, as her immediate predecessors and philosophical mentors make amply clear. The hierarchies it erects are the old ones: Michael Hardt and Toni Negri think it is a good thing that entire populations of peasants and tribals were wiped out because their extermination increased the vital energies of the system as a whole. And if vitalism's hierarchies produce "unnecessary suffering," well, then so do its levelings: Deleuze and Guattari think that French-occupied Africa was an "open social field" where black people showed how sexually liberated they were by fantasizing about "being beaten by a white man."[7]

Option #2:

They could follow the Heideggerian path,
which would require them to show that humanity is a species with weird powers—that
humans (and humans alone) can fundamentally distort the universe's most basic feature
or *hypokeinomon*. That would certainly do the
political trick. Vitalism would doubtless take
on an urgency if it could make the case that
human beings were capable of demateral-
izing vibrant matter—or of making it less vibrant—or of pouring sugar into the gas tank
of Becoming. But Bennett and Connolly are
not going to follow this path either, for the
simple reason that they don't believe anything of the sort. Their books are designed
in large part to attest the opposite—that
humanity has no superpowers, no special
role to play nor even to refuse to play. Early
on, Bennett praises Spinoza for "rejecting
the idea that man 'disturbs rather than follows Nature's order.'" We'll want to note that
Spinoza's claim has no *normative* force; it's a
statement of fact. We don't need to be talked
out of disturbing nature's order, because we
already don't. The same grammatical mood
obtains when Bennett quotes a modern stu-
dent of Spinoza: "human beings do not form
a separate imperium unto themselves."[8] We

"do not"—the claim in its ontological form means *could not*—stand apart and so await no homecoming or reunion.

Those sentences sound entirely settled, but there are other passages in *Vibrant Matter* when you can watch in real time as such claims visibly neutralize the political programs they are being called upon to motivate. Here's Bennett: "My hunch is that the image of dead or thoroughly instrumentalized matter feeds human hubris and our earth-destroying fantasies of conquest and consumption."[9] On a quick read you might think that this is nothing more than a little junk Heideggerianism—that techno-thinking turns the world into a lumberyard, &c. But on closer inspection, the sentence sounds nothing like Heidegger and is, indeed, entirely puzzling. For if it is "hubris" to think that human beings could "conquer and consume" the world—not hubris to do it, but hubris only to *think* it, hubris only in the form of "fantasy"—then in what danger is the earth of actually being destroyed? How could mere imagination have world-negating effects and *still remain imagination*? Bennett's position seems to be that I have to recognize that consuming the world is impossible, because if I don't, I might end up consuming the world. Her argument only gains political traction by crediting the fantasy that she is putatively out to dispel. Or there's this: Bennett doesn't like it when a philosopher, in this instance Hannah Arendt, "positions human intentionality as the most important of all agential factors, the bearer on an exceptional kind of power."[10] Her book's great unanswered question, in this light, is whether she can account for ecological calamity, which is perhaps her central preoccupation, without some notion of human agency as potent and malign, if only in the sense that human beings have the capacity to destroy entire ecosystems and striped bass don't. The incoherence that underlies the new vitalism can thus be telegraphed in two complementary questions: If human beings don't actually possess exceptional power, then why is it important to convince them to adopt a language that attributes to them less of it? But if they do possess such power, then on what grounds do I tell them that their language is wrong?

Option #3
Enlightenment it is, then. What remains, I mean, for both Connolly and Bennett, is the simple idea that most people subscribe to a false ontology and are accordingly in need of re-education. Connolly describes himself and his fellow vitalists as "seers"—he also

calls them "those exquisitely sensitive to the world"—and he more than once quotes Nietzsche referring to everyone else, the non-seers, the foggy-eyed, as "apes."[11] I don't much like being called an orangutan and know others who will like it even less, but at least this rendering of Bennett/Connolly has the possible merit of making the object-world genuinely autonomous and so getting the cosmos out from under the coercions of thought. *Our thinking might affect us, but it cannot affect the universe.* But there is a difficulty even here—the most injurious of political ontology's several problems, I think—which is that via this observation philosophy returns magnetically to its proper object—or non-object—which is thought, and we realize with a start that the only thing that is actually up for grabs in these new realist philosophies of the object is in fact our thinking personhood. This is really quite remarkable. Bennett says that the task facing contemporary philosophy is to "shift from epistemology to ontology," but she herself undertakes the dead opposite. She has precisely misnamed her procedure: "We *are* vital materiality," she writes, "and we are surrounded by it, though we do not always see it that way. The ethical task at hand here is to cultivate the ability to discern nonhuman vitality, to become perceptually open to it."[12] There is nothing about her ontology that Bennett feels she needs to work out; it is entirely given. The philosopher's commission is instead to devise the moralized epistemology that will vindicate this ontology, and which will, in its students, produce "dispositions" or "moods" or, as Connolly has it, a "working upon the self" or the "cultivation of a capacity" or a "sensibility" or maybe even just another intellectual "stance." Connolly and Bennett have lots of language for describing mindsets and almost no language for describing objects. Their arguments take shape almost entirely on the terrain of *Geist*. They really just want to get the subjectivity right.

There are various ways one might bring this betrayal of the object into view, in addition to quoting Bennett and Connolly's plain statements on the matter. Among the great self-defeating deficiencies of these books are the fully pragmatist argumentative procedures adopted by their authors, who adduce no arguments in favor of their chosen ontology. Bennett points out that her position is really just an "experiment" with different ways of "narrating"; an "experiment with an idea"; a "thought experiment," Connolly says. "What would happen to our thinking about nature if…"[13] The post-structuralism that both philosophers think they've put behind them thus survives intact. But such play with discourse is, of course, entirely inconsistent with a robust philosophy of objects, premised as it is on the idea that the object exerts no pressure on the language we use to describe it, which indeed we elect at will. The mind, as convinced of its freedom as it ever was, chooses a philosophical idiom just to *see what it can do.*

This problem—the problem, I mean of an object-philosophy that can't stop talking about the subject—then redoubles itself in two ways:

1. The problem is redoubled, first, in the blank epiphanies of Bennett's prose style, and especially when she makes like Novalis on the streets of Baltimore, putting in front of readers an assemblage of objects the author encountered beneath a highway underpass so that we can imagine ourselves beside her watching them pulsate. The problem is that she literally tells us nothing about these items except that she heard them chime. One begins to say that she chose four particular objects—a glove, pollen, a dead rat, and a bottle cap—except that formulation is already misleading, since lacking further description, these four objects aren't particular

at all. They are sham specificities, for which any other four objects could have served just as well. She could have changed any or all of them—could have improvised any Borgesian quartet—and she could have written the page in *exactly the same manner*. You can suggest your own, like this:

- a sock, some leaves, a lame squirrel, and a soda can
- a castoff T-shirt, a fallen tree limb, a hungry kitten, and an empty Cheetos bag
- a bowler hat, a beehive, a grimy parasol, and Idi Amin

These aren't objects; these are *slots*; and Bennett's procedure is to that extent entirely abstract. This is what it means to say that materialism, too, is just another philosophy of the subject. It does no more or less than any other intellectual system, maintaining the word "object" only as a vacancy onto which to project its good intentions.

ii. The problem is redoubled, second, in the nakedly religious idiom in which these two books solemnize their arguments. That idiom, indeed, is really just pragmatism in cassock and cope. The final page of Bennett's book prints a "Nicene Creed for would-be vital materialists." Connolly's book begins by offering its readers "good tidings." Nor does the latter build arguments or gather evidence; instead, he "confesses" a "philosophy/faith," which is also a "faith/conviction," which is also a "philosophy/creed."[14] Bennett and Connolly hold vespers for the teeming world. Eager young materialists, turning to these books to help round out their still developing views, must be at least somewhat alarmed to discover that our relationship to matter is actually one of "faith" or "conviction." A philosophical account of the object is replaced by a pledge—a deferral—a promise, by definition tentative, offered in a mood of expectancy, to take the object on trust. Nor is this in any way a gotcha point. Connolly is completely open about his (Deleuzian) aim "to restore belief in the world."[15] It's just that no sooner is this aim uttered than the world undergoes the fate of anything in which we believe, since if you name your belief as belief, then you are conceding that your position is optional and to some considerable degree unfounded and that you do not, in that sense, believe it at all.

It's not difficult, at any rate, to show that Connolly for one does not believe in his own book. The stated purpose of *A World of Becoming* is to show us how to "affirm" that

117

condition.[16] That's really all that's left for us to do, once one has determined that Becoming will go on becoming even without our help and even if we work against it. Connolly's writing, it should be said, is generally short on case studies or named examples of emergent conjunctures, leaving readers to guess what exactly they are being asked to affirm. For many chapters on end, one gets the impression that the only important way in which the world is currently becoming is that more people from Somalia are moving to the Netherlands, and that the phrase "people who resist Becoming" is really just Connolly's idiosyncratically metaphysical synonym for "racists." But near the end of book three concrete examples do appear, all at once—three Acts of Becoming—two completed, one still in train: the 2003 invasion of Iraq; the 2008 financial collapse; and global warming. All three seem, in some sufficiently vague way, to confirm the vitalist position in that they have been transformative and destabilizing and will for the foreseeable future produce unpredictable and ramifying consequences. What is surprising—but then really, no, finally not the least bit surprising—is that Connolly uses a word in regard to these three cases that a Nietzschean committed to boundless affirmation shouldn't be able to write: "warning."[17] Melting icecaps are not to be affirmed—that's Connolly's own view of the matter. Mass foreclosure is not to be affirmed. Quite the contrary: If you know that the cosmos is capable of shifting suddenly, then you might be able to get the word out. The responsibility borne by philosophers' shifts from affirmation to its opposite: Vitalists can caution others about what rushes on. The philosopher of Becoming thus asks us to celebrate transformation only until he runs up against the first change he doesn't like.

This is tough to take in. Lots of things are missing from political ontology: politics, objects, an intelligible metaphilosophy. But surely one had the right to expect from a theorist of systemic and irreversible change, one with politics on his mind, some reminder of the possibility of revolution, some evocation, since evocations remain needful, of the joy of that mutation, the elation reserved for those moments when Event overtakes Circumstance. But in Connolly, where one might have glimpsed the grinning disbelief of experience unaccounted for, one finds only the killing fields of Diyala, hence fear, hence the old determination to fight the future. The philosopher of fire grabs the extinguisher. The philosopher of water walks in with a mop.

[1] See Connolly, William, World of Becoming, Durham, Duke University Press, 2011, p. 16.

[2] Bennett, Jane, Vibrant Matter: A Political Ecology of Things, Durham, Duke University Press, 2010

[3] See Connolly, William, Neuropolitics: Thinking, Culture, Speed, Minneapolis, University of Minnesota Press, 2002

[4] Kaufmann and "agency", p. 21; "complexity," p. 56; "mystics," p. 68. in Connolly, William, World of Becoming, Durham, Duke University Press, 2011

[5] Bennett, Jane, Vibrant Matter: A Political Ecology of Things, Durham, Duke University Press, 2010, p. 12; 13.

[6] Heidegger, Martin, "Letter on Humanism", 1947, Heidegger's Basic Writings, New York, Harper & Row, 1977, p. 190-242.

[7] Hardt and Negri praise the United States' "Open Frontiers" in Empire, p. 168-173; Deleuze and Guattari devise a Senegal of their own imagining on p. 96 of Anti-Oedipus, 1972, trans. Robert Hurley, Mark Seem, and Helen Lane, Minneapolis, Univ. of Minnesota, 1983.

[8] Bennett, p. x; quoting Nancy Levene, p. 2. in Vibrant Matter: A Political Ecology of Things

[9] Ibid., p. ix.

[10] Ibid., p. 34.

[11] Connolly: Chapter 6 is called "The Theorist and the Seer"; "exquisitely sensitive," p. 69; "apes," e.g., p. 169, in World of Becoming, Durham, Duke University Press, 2011

[12] Bennett, Vibrant Matter: A Political Ecology of Things, p. 3 & p. 14.

[13] Ibid., p. 62 and 69; Connolly, p. 170.

[14] Bennett, p. 122; Connolly, p. 16; 37; 39.

[15] Connolly, p. 61.

[16] Ibid., p. 79.

[17] Ibid. p. 155.

Towards A Realist Pan-Constructivism

Levi Bryant

One of my worries about the new turn towards realism is that it will end up washing away all of the valuable social critiques that arose out of Marxist thought, the early Frankfurt School, structuralist, post-structuralist, feminist, queer, and race theory. In particular, I worry that situating these discussions *abstractly* as debates between monolithic positions of "realism" and "anti-realism", deeply risks ignoring the *ontological specificity* of the field out of which social constructivist positions arose and the political and ethical considerations that have motivated these positions. It also, I believe, risks glossing over unique ontological features of humans and social systems, oddly shifting away from a "realist" position (i.e., one would think that realism is particularly attentive to the genuine ontological features of entities). When I hear questions at conferences about where the place of feminism, post-colonial theory, and queer theory is in Object Oriented Ontology responded to with the claim that "maybe we need to stop worry-

122

ing about these things", I find myself deeply disturbed. I find myself disturbed because 1) I think variants of OOO are capable of addressing these issues in a satisfying way[1], and 2) because I think we *can't* ignore these issues. The forms of oppression that arise from essentialist conceptions of human "types" continue to have very real consequences for human lives as well as play a key role in perpetuating capitalist systems of exploitation that both cause misery for billions of people and are destroying the planet. If Speculative Realism simply turns away from these things out of a zeal for defeating anti-realism, then it has little to offer for concrete struggles around the world.

Nonetheless, for me, at least, there were very real political and ethical reasons for turning to a realist/materialist position. It wasn't because I had suddenly abandoned the lessons I had learned during my anti-realist days from theorists such as Lacan, Zizek, Butler, Foucault, Adorno, Derrida, Baudrillard, etc., it was because I increasingly began to experience the *limits* of these positions with respect to the problems we face today. Encountering the limits of something is quite different from rejecting that thing. To reject something is to banish it entirely from one's theoretical edifice as in the case of the theory of the humors banished as an explanation of sickness, or phlogiston banished as an explanation for why things burn. Encountering the limits of something, by contrast, entails that one *retains* the theoretical advances of that thing, while also recognizing that there are a broad body of things this theory does not explain. In such a moment one recognizes that one's ontology needs to be expanded to cover entirely new domains that exceed those of the field of investigation in the previous domain. This is the moment where one recognizes that a new discipline needs to be forged (and no I'm not making the pretentious claim that *I'm* forging a new discipline). This is what happened with me and anti-realism. It wasn't that I had somehow come to reject Adorno's reflections on the culture industry, Foucault's analysis of epistemes in the social sciences, Butler's reflections on the construction of gender, post-structuralist accounts of the construction of race, Marx's critique of commodity-fetishism, etc. No, as I make clear in the introduction to *The Democracy of Objects*, I continue to endorse these accounts as I always did. Indeed, one of the reasons I chose Luhmann's account of the autopoiesis of objects was that it was the most radical account of *constructivism* I was familiar with and was therefore capable of *integrating* these lines of argument.[2]

Rather, what I discovered was that the Lacanian axiom I had advocated for so many years– that "the universe is the flower of rhetoric"[3] –was *limited* in its ability to respond to the problems that were of importance to me. Marx was an adequate theoretical framework for thinking the dynamics of global capital. Thinkers like Zizek and Adorno were adequate for thinking ideology. Thinkers like Lacan and Deleuze and Guattari (though I think D&G are realists) were adequate for thinking desire. Thinkers like Foucault were adequate for thinking about how institutions and scientific discourses in the social sciences discursively and through power produce subjects. Thinkers like Baudrillard and Bourdieu were adequate for explaining why certain objects take on cultural value. Thinkers like Butler were adequate for thinking the social construction of gender. Etc.

Yet none of these things were adequate for thinking problems like climate change, the impact of technologies on the world, or the impact of geography on social formations. If you're going to think seriously about things like climate change, for example, discussions of lived experience or how "the universe is the flower of rhetoric" will not do. You need to take seriously *real properties* of greenhouse gases, the earth's albedo, methane gases released from garbage dumps, cow farts, diets, the flight of people from the cities to the suburbs and how automobiles made this possible, fluctuations in the sun's output, ocean temperatures, etc. Analyses of lived experience or the social construction of objects are thoroughly inadequate for responding to these things. At some point you need to hang your hat on the peg and recognize that you're not just talking about *discourses* or *signifiers*. Yes, yes, you want to talk about discourses, texts, and signifiers *too*. Yes, yes, you want to talk about lived experience *too*. But this is not *enough*. You need to take into account the mind, language, and sign independence of these beings as well. There's no way around this. At least, I don't think there's any way around this.

I want to have my social constructivism and have my realism too. In fact, I want to go so far in my realism that I even count *social constructions as real*. They are all too real for those who live with their negative effects and like an ecosystem they regulate the possibilities of lives, our ability to respond to pressing problems like climate change, and the lives of countless nonhuman beings. However, recognizing that a theoretical framework is *limited* and that more theoretical work needs to be done broaching different domains of analysis does not leave the original theory *unchanged*.

In *The Democracy of Objects* I claim that I'm able to integrate the findings of Zizek.[4] I have been described as a psychotic by some detractors because I treat words like things, and it has been argued that I can't really integrate Zizek unless I embrace his Hegelianism. We must remember that 1) Freud describes the psychotic as revealing on the surface the truth of the unconscious[5] and 2) in his final teaching Lacan described *himself* as a psychotic and praised Joyce for finding a non-Oedipal solution in the case of his own psychosis.[6] I'd say I'm in good company, especially for those who have understood the argument of *Anti-Oedipus* (which Lacan, incidentally, praised)!

Finally, I would argue that we must understand the difference between the letter and the signifier in Lacan. The letter refers to a sheer material inscription in the unconscious without sense or meaning that nonetheless produces various effects of meaning in the form of puns, homonyms, equivokes and so on. Here we encounter the thingliness of the unconscious that produces effects of sense out of nonsense; we encounter "words" as things.[7]

Integration doesn't entail sublation of *all* elements of a theoretical edifice. Theoretical changes, even where they don't reject all elements of the previous theoretical edifice, do not leave that previous theoretical edifice unchanged. Things need to be reworked in light of the new additions. Other claims need to be abandoned. New elements need to be introduced into the previous theory. The previous theory, while not rejected, is not the same as it was before. And this is how it is with Zizek's Hegelianism. I believe that I can integrate the framework of Lacanian theory of the subject, desire, and jouissance within a Luhmannian framework of sociological autopoietic theory, but this is a far cry from endorsing the claim that there is an identity of substance and subject. No, the whole point of the realist move with respect to problems like climate change was that we can no longer claim that signifying articulations are the structuring agency of all being. We can no longer say that "reality is a synthesis of the imaginary and the symbolic". [8] No, reality has to become something closer to the Lacanian *real*, and the Hegelian real is something that evades all dialectical sublation, even the fraught, contradictory, Goedelian, and open sublation that Zizek advocates. At best Zizek gives us a nuanced version of commodity fetishism. But there's more to heaven and earth than commodity fetishism. In this framework, all sorts of things, following Guattari, would have to be included in the Lacanian framework that tend to be ignored: the literal architecture of the institution where the clinic is practiced, the relations between the people that are there, the sort of work that is done by "patients" and "analysts", the media used, artistic practices, economics, the material sociological setting of the neighborhood, etc., etc., etc. *In addition to the signifier*, we would have to attend to the role these things play.

To recognize the limits of a theory is also to recognize the limitations of a theory or the *domain to which it is limited*. Whitehead famously said that the shortcomings of a theory are not generally the result of outright false claims or logically incoherent arguments, but rather *overstatement*.[9] A philosophy or theory discovers something that is *true* of the world and the next thing you know, like an obsessional man whose partner has told him that something "works" for him or her, he repeatedly tries to do the same thing over and over again in the bedroom making it unbearable. Recognizing the limitations of a theory thus means recognizing the domain to which it is limited, the domain where it "works", but also being open to the domain beyond this where other theoretical tools are needed. Over time the social constructivists became like the obsessional man in the bedroom. In their meditations on social construction they had found something *true* and *real*, but the next thing you knew they were trying to apply this discovery *everywhere* and *always*, ignoring everything else. Suddenly everything was socially constructed and there was nothing outside of social construction. And, of course, as we all know, what began as something valuable and pleasurable, becomes in these circumstances something painful and destructive. Ian Hacking, I think, provides us with the means of retaining the truth of social constructivism while also recognizing its limits. In *The Social Construction of What?* Hacking distinguishes between *interactive* and non-interactive concepts.[10] His thesis is that the social constructivists are speaking of interactive concepts when they speak of social construction. What, then, is an interactive concept or category? An interactive category is a category in which the people named by the category can be *affected* by the category. When a person is diagnosed by a family practitioner as an alcoholic, that category is not simply a *description* but rather 1) the person so defined can adopt behaviors and thoughts in accord with the category, and 2) the category can change their social relations. The person defined by the doctor as an alcoholic might, for example, begin to draw on cultural narratives about what alcoholics are like– for example, the film *Leaving Las Vegas* –and begin to enact those behaviors where they didn't before. Likewise, the person's social relations can change as in the case where the doctor's diagnosis has legal ramifications, leading them to be forced into some form of treatment or even sent to an institution. Here it's worth remembering that these sorts of categories aren't simply a *personal* affair, but rather are a *collective* affair.

The point is that unlike rocks, persons and social systems *interact* with the categories that befall them. They take up attitudes and behaviors with respect to these categories. It is in this sense that people and social institutions are formed or constructed by signifiers and concepts. A media report that says the economy is bad is not simply a *description* of the economy, but becomes a call to action upon economic institutions, governments, and individual people regardless of whether its true. By contrast, rocks adopt no attitude or behavior with respect to the way we categorize them. They go on behaving rockishly just as they always did before. The important point is that these categorizations are not simply a matter of us adopting an attitude pro or con with respect to how we individually have been categorized. Rather, these categories function *independent* of us, socially, even where we think they're bullshit. The former Republican US Presidential candidate Herman Cain might think that racial categorizations are bullshit and that we're all free neoliberal subjects, but the social system still codes him in ways to which he must respond. Even where he doesn't adopt an attitude towards these things, the effect of these signifying structures still has a causal impact on him that delimit possibilities for him, that situate him socially in such a way, and that contribute to his life experiences and how he develops.

My point is that if we're true realists– and hopefully materialists! –we should be attentive to the properties of different types of systems. We should recognize those systems that have capacities of reflexivity or of taking up attitudes towards ways in which they are described and those systems that do not have these characteristics. And given this we should heartily embrace theories of social constructivism, recognizing that categorizations and signifying structures have a real impact on the operations of reflexive systems leading them to develop in particular way. It does not have to be an either/or where we're forced to choose between lived experience and semiosis or the real effect of cow farts on climate. Rather, it should be a both/and where we recognize that for certain types of systems descriptions have real constructive effects and for other types of systems descriptions do not. We should be able to have our Baudrillardian analysis of the system of objects as commodities imbued with symbolic value and our realism too.

[1] For an object-oriented framework that integrates these sorts of questions and modes of analysis, cf. Bryant, Levi R., The Democracy of Objects, Ann Arbor, Open Humanities Press, 2012, Introduction & chap. 4.

[2] Luhmann, Niklas "The Cognitive Program of Constructivism and the Reality That Remains Unknown", in Theories of Distinction: Redescribing the Descriptions of Modernity, ed. William Rasch, Stanford, Stanford University Press, 2002, and Niklas Luhmann, Social Systems, trans. John Bednarz, Jr and Dirk Baeker, Stanford, Stanford University Press, 1995.

[3] Lacan, Jacques, "Encore: On Femine Sexuality", The Limits of Love and Knowledge, trans. Bruce Fink,

New York, W.W. Norton & Co, 1998, p. 56.

[4] Bryant, Levi R., The Democracy of Objects, section 3.5

[5] Freud, Sigmund, "The Unconscious", in The Standard Edition of the Complete Psychological Works of Sigmund Freud, Vol 14, ed. James Strachey, New York, Vintage, 2001, p. 197 – 204

[6] Lacan, Jacques, The Sinthome: Seminar 23, trans. Cormac Gallagher, unpublished seminar

[7] Lacan, Jacques, "Encore: On Femine Sexuality", chap. 3

[8] Lacan, Jacques, Seminar 11: The Four Fundamental Concepts of Psychoanalysis, trans. Alan Sheridan, New York, W.W. Norton & Co., 1997, p. 53 – 60

[9] Whitehead, Alfred North, Process and Reality, ed. David Ray Griffin and Donald W. Sherburne, New York, The Free Press, 1978, p. 7

[10] Hacking, Ian, The Social Construction of What?, Cambridge, Harvard University Press, 1999, p. 31 – 32

#Accelerate Manifesto for an Accelerationist Politics

Nick Srnicek and Alex Williams

01. INTRODUCTION: On the Conjuncture

1. At the beginning of the second decade of the Twenty-First Century, global civilization faces a new breed of cataclysm. These coming apocalypses ridicule the norms and organisational structures of the politics which were forged in the birth of the nation-state, the rise of capitalism, and a Twentieth Century of unprecedented wars.

2. Most significant is the breakdown of the planetary climatic system. In time, this threatens the continued existence of the present global human population. Though this is the most critical of the threats which face humanity, a series of lesser but potentially equally destabilising problems exist alongside and intersect with it. Terminal resource depletion, especially in water and energy reserves, offers the prospect of mass starvation, collapsing economic paradigms, and new hot and cold wars. Continued finan-

cial crisis has led governments to embrace the paralyzing death spiral policies of austerity, privatisation of social welfare services, mass unemployment, and stagnating wages. Increasing automation in production processes—including 'intellectual labour'—is evidence of the secular crisis of capitalism, soon to render it incapable of maintaining current standards of living for even the former middle classes of the global north.

3. In contrast to these ever-accelerating catastrophes, today's politics is beset by an inability to generate the new ideas and modes of organisation necessary to transform our societies to confront and resolve the coming annihilations. While crisis gathers force and speed, politics withers and retreats. In this paralysis of the political imaginary, the future has been cancelled.

4. Since 1979, the hegemonic global political ideology has been neoliberalism, found in some variant throughout the leading economic powers. In spite of the deep structural challenges the new global problems present to it, most immediately the credit, financial, and fiscal crises since 2007-8, neoliberal programmes have only evolved in the sense of deepening. This continuation of the neoliberal project, or neoliberalism 2.0, has

begun to apply another round of structural adjustments, most significantly in the form of encouraging new and aggressive incursions by the private sector into what remains of social democratic institutions and services. This is in spite of the immediately negative economic and social effects of such policies, and the longer term fundamental barriers posed by the new global crises.

5. That the forces of right wing governmental, non-governmental, and corporate power have been able to press forth with neoliberalisation is at least in part a result of the continued paralysis and ineffectual nature of much what remains of the left. Thirty years of neoliberalism have rendered most left-leaning political parties bereft of radical thought, hollowed out, and without a popular mandate. At best they have responded to our present crises with calls for a return to a Keynesian economics, in spite of the evidence that the very conditions which enabled post-war social democracy to occur no longer exist. We cannot return to mass industrial-Fordist labour by fiat, if at all. Even the neosocialist regimes of South America's Bolivarian Revolution, whilst heartening in their ability to resist the dogmas of contemporary capitalism, remain disappointingly unable to advance an alternative beyond

mid-Twentieth Century socialism. Organised labour, being systematically weakened by the changes wrought in the neoliberal project, is sclerotic at an institutional level and—at best—capable only of mildly mitigating the new structural adjustments. But with no systematic approach to building a new economy, or the structural solidarity to push such changes through, for now labour remains relatively impotent. The new social movements which emerged since the end of the Cold War, experiencing a resurgence in the years after 2008, have been similarly unable to devise a new political ideological vision. Instead they expend considerable energy on internal direct-democratic process and affective self-valorisation over strategic efficacy, and frequently propound a variant of neo-primitivist localism, as if to oppose the abstract violence of globalised capital with the flimsy and ephemeral "authenticity" of communal immediacy.

6. In the absence of a radically new social, political, organisational, and economic vision the hegemonic powers of the right will continue to be able to push forward their narrow-minded imaginary, in the face of any and all evidence. At best, the left may be able for a time to partially resist some of the worst incursions. But this is to be Canute

against an ultimately irresistible tide. To generate a new left global hegemony entails a recovery of lost possible futures, and indeed the recovery of *the future* as such.

02. INTEREGNUM: On Accelerationisms

1. If any system has been associated with ideas of acceleration it is capitalism. The essential metabolism of capitalism demands economic growth, with competition between individual capitalist entities setting in motion increasing technological developments in an attempt to achieve competitive advantage, all accompanied by increasing social dislocation. In its neoliberal form, its ideological self-presentation is one of liberating the forces of creative destruction, setting free ever-accelerating technological and social innovations.

2. The philosopher Nick Land captured this most acutely, with a myopic yet hypnotising belief that capitalist speed alone could generate a global transition towards unparalleled technological singularity. In this visioning of capital, the human can eventually be discarded as mere drag to an abstract planetary intelligence rapidly constructing itself from the bricolaged fragments

of former civilisations. However Landian neoliberalism confuses speed with acceleration. We may be moving fast, but only within a strictly defined set of capitalist parameters that themselves never waver. We experience only the increasing speed of a local horizon, a simple brain-dead onrush rather than an acceleration which is also navigational, an experimental process of discovery within a universal space of possibility. It is the latter mode of acceleration which we hold as essential.

3. Even worse, as Deleuze and Guattari recognized, from the very beginning what capitalist speed deterritorializes with one hand, it reterritorializes with the other. Progress becomes constrained within a framework of surplus value, a reserve army of labour, and free-floating capital. Modernity is reduced to statistical measures of economic growth and social innovation becomes encrusted with kitsch remainders from our communal past. Thatcherite-Reaganite deregulation sits comfortably alongside Victorian 'back-to-basics' family and religious values.

4. A deeper tension within neoliberalism is in terms of its self-image as the vehicle of modernity, as literally synonymous with modernisation, whilst promising a future

that it is constitutively incapable of providing. Indeed, as neoliberalism has progressed, rather than enabling individual creativity, it has tended towards eliminating cognitive inventiveness in favour of an affective production line of scripted interactions, coupled to global supply chains and a neo-Fordist Eastern production zone. A vanishingly small cognitariat of elite intellectual workers shrinks with each passing year – and increasingly so as algorithmic automation winds its way through the spheres of affective and intellectual labour. Neoliberalism, though positing itself as a necessary historical development, was in fact a merely contingent means to ward off the crisis of value that emerged in the 1970s. Inevitably this was a sublimation of the crisis rather than its ultimate overcoming.

5. It is Marx, along with Land, who remains the paradigmatic accelerationist thinker. Contrary to the all-too familiar critique, and even the behaviour of some contemporary Marxians, we must remember that Marx himself used the most advanced theoretical tools and empirical data available in an attempt to fully understand and transform his world. He was not a thinker who resisted modernity, but rather one who sought to analyse and intervene within it, understand-

ing that for all its exploitation and corruption, capitalism remained the most advanced economic system to date. Its gains were not to be reversed, but accelerated beyond the constraints the capitalist value form.

6. Indeed, as even Lenin wrote in the 1918 text *"Left Wing" Childishness*:

> Socialism is inconceivable without large-scale capitalist engineering based on the latest discoveries of modern science. It is inconceivable without planned state organisation which keeps tens of millions of people to the strictest observance of a unified standard in production and distribution. We Marxists have always spoken of this, and it is not worth while wasting two seconds talking to people who do not understand even this (anarchists and a good half of the Left Socialist-Revolutionaries).

7. As Marx was aware, capitalism cannot be identified as the agent of true acceleration. Similarly, the assessment of left politics as antithetical to technosocial acceleration is also, at least in part, a severe misrepresentation. Indeed, if the political left is to have a future it must be one in which it maximally embraces this suppressed accelerationist tendency.

03: MANIFEST: On the Future

1. We believe the most important division in today's left is between those that hold to a *folk politics* of localism, direct action, and relentless horizontalism, and those that outline what must become called an *accelerationist politics* at ease with a modernity of abstraction, complexity, globality, and technology. The former remains content with establishing small and temporary spaces of non-capitalist social relations, eschewing the real problems entailed in facing foes which are intrinsically non-local, abstract, and rooted deep in our everyday infrastructure. The failure of such politics has been built-in from the very beginning. By contrast, an accelerationist politics seeks to preserve the gains of late capitalism while going further than its value system, governance structures, and mass pathologies will allow.

2. All of us want to work less. It is an intriguing question as to why it was that the world's leading economist of the post-war era believed that an enlightened capitalism inevitably progressed towards a radical reduction of working hours. In *The Economic Prospects for Our Grandchildren* (written in 1930), Keynes forecast a capitalist future where individuals would have their work reduced to three

hours a day. What has instead occurred is the progressive elimination of the work-life distinction, with work coming to permeate every aspect of the emerging social factory.

3. Capitalism has begun to constrain the productive forces of technology, or at least, direct them towards needlessly narrow ends. Patent wars and idea monopolisation are contemporary phenomena that point to both capital's need to move beyond competition, and capital's increasingly retrograde approach to technology. The properly accelerative gains of neoliberalism have not led to less work or less stress. And rather than a world of space travel, future shock, and revolutionary technological potential, we exist in a time where the only thing which develops is marginally better consumer gadgetry. Relentless iterations of the same basic product sustain marginal consumer demand at the expense of human acceleration.

4. We do not want to return to Fordism. There can be no return to Fordism. The capitalist "golden era" was premised on the production paradigm of the orderly factory environment, where (male) workers received security and a basic standard of living in return for a lifetime of stultifying boredom and social repression. Such a system relied

upon an international hierarchy of colonies, empires, and an underdeveloped periphery; a national hierarchy of racism and sexism; and a rigid family hierarchy of female subjugation. For all the nostalgia many may feel, this regime is both undesirable and practically impossible to return to.

5. Accelerationists want to unleash latent productive forces. In this project, the material platform of neoliberalism does not need to be destroyed. It needs to be *repurposed* towards common ends. The existing infrastructure is not a capitalist stage to be smashed, but a springboard to launch towards post-capitalism.

6. Given the enslavement of technoscience to capitalist objectives (especially since the late 1970s) we surely do not yet know what a modern technosocial body can do. Who amongst us fully recognizes what untapped potentials await in the technology which has already been developed? Our wager is that the true transformative potentials of much of our technological and scientific research remain unexploited, filled with presently redundant features (or *pre-adaptations*) that, following a shift beyond the short-sighted capitalist socius, can become decisive.

7. We want to accelerate the process of technological evolution. But what we are arguing for is not techno-utopianism. Never believe that technology will be *sufficient* to save us. Necessary, yes, but never sufficient without socio-political action. Technology and the social are intimately bound up with one another, and changes in either potentiate and reinforce changes in the other. Whereas the techno-utopians argue for acceleration on the basis that it will automatically overcome social conflict, our position is that technology should be accelerated precisely because it is needed in order to *win* social conflicts.

8. We believe that any post-capitalism will require post-capitalist planning. The faith placed in the idea that, after a revolution, the people will spontaneously constitute a novel socioeconomic system that isn't simply a return to capitalism is naïve at best, and ignorant at worst. To further this, we must develop both a cognitive map of the existing system and a speculative image of the future economic system.

9. To do so, the left must take advantage of every technological and scientific advance made possible by capitalist society. We declare that quantification is not an evil to be eliminated, but a tool to be used in the most

effective manner possible. Economic modelling is – simply put – a necessity for making intelligible a complex world. The 2008 financial crisis reveals the risks of blindly accepting mathematical models on faith, yet this is a problem of illegitimate authority not of mathematics itself. The tools to be found in social network analysis, agent-based modelling, big data analytics, and non-equilibrium economic models, are necessary cognitive mediators for understanding complex systems like the modern economy. The accelerationist left must become literate in these technical fields.

10. Any transformation of society must involve economic and social experimentation. The Chilean Project Cybersyn is emblematic of this experimental attitude – fusing advanced cybernetic technologies, with sophisticated economic modelling, and a democratic platform instantiated in the technological infrastructure itself. Similar experiments were conducted in 1950s-1960s Soviet economics as well, employing cybernetics and linear programming in an attempt to overcome the new problems faced by the first communist economy. That both of these were ultimately unsuccessful can be traced to the political and technological constraints these early cyberneticians operated under.

11. The left must develop sociotechnical hegemony: both in the sphere of ideas, and in the sphere of material platforms. Platforms are the infrastructure of global society. They establish the basic parameters of what is possible, both behaviourally and ideologically. In this sense, they embody the material transcendental of society: they are what make possible particular sets of actions, relationships, and powers. While much of the current global platform is biased towards capitalist social relations, this is not an inevitable necessity. These material platforms of production, finance, logistics, and consumption can and will be reprogrammed and reformatted towards post-capitalist ends.

12. We do not believe that direct action is sufficient to achieve any of this. The habitual tactics of marching, holding signs, and establishing temporary autonomous zones risk becoming comforting substitutes for effective success. "At least we have done *something*" is the rallying cry of those who privilege self-esteem rather than effective action. The only criterion of a good tactic is whether it enables significant success or not. We must be done with fetishising particular modes of action. Politics must be treated as a set of dynamic systems, riven with conflict,

adaptations and counter-adaptations, and strategic arms races. This means that each individual type of political action becomes blunted and ineffective over time as the other sides adapt. No given mode of political action is historically inviolable. Indeed, over time, there is an increasing need to discard familiar tactics as the forces and entities they are marshalled against learn to defend and counter-attack them effectively. It is in part the contemporary left's inability to do so which lies close to the heart of the contemporary malaise.

13. The overwhelming privileging of democracy-as-process needs to be left behind. The fetishisation of openness, horizontality, and inclusion of much of today's 'radical' left set the stage for ineffectiveness. Secrecy, verticality, and exclusion all have their place as well in effective political action (though not, of course, an exclusive one).

14. Democracy cannot be defined simply by its means – not via voting, discussion, or general assemblies. Real democracy must be defined by its goal – collective self-mastery. This is a project which must align politics with the legacy of the Enlightenment, to the extent that it is only through harnessing our ability to understand ourselves and our

world better (our social, technical, economic, psychological world) that we can come to rule ourselves. We need to posit a collectively controlled legitimate vertical authority *in addition* to distributed horizontal forms of sociality, to avoid becoming the slaves of either a tyrannical totalitarian centralism or a capricious emergent order beyond our control. The command of The Plan must be married to the improvised order of The Network.

15. We do not present any particular organisation as the ideal means to embody these vectors. What is needed – what has always been needed – is an ecology of organisations, a pluralism of forces, resonating and feeding back on their comparative strengths. Sectarianism is the death knell of the left as much as centralization is, and in this regard we continue to welcome experimentation with different tactics (even those we disagree with).

16. We have three medium term concrete goals. First, we need to build an intellectual infrastructure. Mimicking the Mont Pelerin Society of the neoliberal revolution, this is to be tasked with creating a new ideology, economic and social models, and a vision of the good to replace and surpass the emaciated ideals that rule our world today. This

is an infrastructure in the sense of requiring the construction not just of ideas, but institutions and material paths to inculcate, embody and spread them.

17. We need to construct wide-scale media reform. In spite of the seeming democratisation offered by the internet and social media, traditional media outlets remain crucial in the selection and framing of narratives, along with possessing the funds to prosecute investigative journalism. Bringing these bodies as close as possible to popular control is crucial to undoing the current presentation of the state of things.

18. Finally, we need to reconstitute various forms of class power. Such a reconstitution must move beyond the notion that an organically generated global proletariat already exists. Instead it must seek to knit together a disparate array of partial proletarian identities, often embodied in post-Fordist forms of precarious labour.

19. Groups and individuals are already at work on each of these, but each is on their own insufficient. What is required is all three feeding back into one another, with each modifying the contemporary conjunction in such a way that the others become more

and more effective. A positive feedback loop of infrastructural, ideological, social and economic transformation, generating a new complex hegemony, a new post-capitalist technosocial platform. History demonstrates it has always been a broad assemblage of tactics and organisations which has brought about systematic change; these lessons must be learned.

20. To achieve each of these goals, on the most practical level we hold that the accelerationist left must think more seriously about the flows of resources and money required to build an effective new political infrastructure. Beyond the 'people power' of bodies in the street, we require funding, whether from governments, institutions, think tanks, unions, or individual benefactors. We consider the location and conduction of such funding flows essential to begin reconstructing an ecology of effective accelerationist left organizations.

21. We declare that only a Promethean politics of maximal mastery over society and its environment is capable of either dealing with global problems or achieving victory over capital. This mastery must be distinguished from that beloved of thinkers of the original Enlightenment. The clockwork

universe of Laplace, so easily mastered given sufficient information, is long gone from the agenda of serious scientific understanding. But this is not to align ourselves with the tired residue of postmodernity, decrying mastery as proto-fascistic or authority as innately illegitimate. Instead we propose that the problems besetting our planet and our species oblige us to refurbish mastery in a newly complex guise; whilst we cannot predict the precise result of our actions, we can determine probabilistically likely ranges of outcomes. What must be coupled to such complex systems analysis is a new form of action: improvisatory and capable of executing a design through a practice which works with the contingencies it discovers only in the course of its acting, in a politics of geosocial artistry and cunning rationality. A form of abductive experimentation that seeks the best means to act in a complex world.

22. We need to revive the argument that was traditionally made for post-capitalism: not only is capitalism an unjust and perverted system, but it is also a system that holds back progress. Our technological development is being suppressed by capitalism, as much as it has been unleashed. Accelerationism is the basic belief that these capacities can

and should be let loose by moving beyond the limitations imposed by capitalist society. The movement towards a surpassing of our current constraints must include more than simply a struggle for a more rational global society. We believe it must also include recovering the dreams which transfixed many from the middle of the Nineteenth Century until the dawn of the neoliberal era, of the quest of Homo Sapiens towards expansion beyond the limitations of the earth and our immediate bodily forms. These visions are today viewed as relics of a more innocent moment. Yet they both diagnose the staggering lack of imagination in our own time, and offer the promise of a future that is affectively invigorating, as well as intellectually energising. After all, it is only a post-capitalist society, made possible by an accelerationist politics, which will ever be capable of delivering on the promissory note of the mid-Twentieth Century's space programmes, to shift beyond a world of minimal technical upgrades towards all-encompassing change. Towards a time of collective self-mastery, and the properly alien future that entails and enables. Towards a completion of the Enlightenment project of self-criticism and self-mastery, rather than its elimination.

23. The choice facing us is severe: either a globalised post-capitalism or a slow fragmentation towards primitivism, perpetual crisis, and planetary ecological collapse.

24. The future needs to be constructed. It has been demolished by neoliberal capitalism and reduced to a cut-price promise of greater inequality, conflict, and chaos. This collapse in the idea of the future is symptomatic of the regressive historical status of our age, rather than, as cynics across the political spectrum would have us believe, a sign of sceptical maturity. What accelerationism pushes towards is a future that is *more modern* – an alternative modernity that neoliberalism is inherently unable to generate. The future must be cracked open once again, unfastening our horizons towards the universal possibilities of the Outside.